Know Your Dreams,
Know Your Self

Know Your

Know Yo

—A

Dreams,
ur Self

Workbook

By Pat & Jim Fregia
with Pat Bonney Shepherd

Celestial Arts / Berkeley, California

Celestial Arts
P.O. Box 7123
Berkeley, CA 94707

Library of Congress Cataloging-in-Publication Data

Fregia, Pat
    Know your dreams, know your self : a workbook / by Pat & Jim Fregia,
with Pat Bonney Shepherd.
        p.   cm.
    Includes bibliographical references.
    ISBN 0-89087-735-1
    1. Dreams. 2. Dream interpretation. I. Fregia, Jim.
II. Shepherd, Pat Bonney. III. Title
    BF1091.F74 1994   94-29883
    154.6'3—dc20   CIP

FIRST PRINTING 1994

1 2 3 4 5 – 98 97 96 95 94

With Appreciation...

❦ from Pat Fregia to:

*My parents: my father who taught me to follow
my intuition and my mother who had faith and gave
encouragement even without understanding*

❦ from Pat and Jim Fregia to:

*Pat Shepherd, for responding to a divine appointment
the three of us made somewhere in time, and for
her patience and perseverance in deciphering and
clarifying information*

❦ from Pat Shepherd to:

*My husband, Bill, for the kind of unconditional love
and support most of us dream about but few of us
experience past the age of two, and my daughter,
Karen, for wisdom far beyond her youth*

*Pat and Jim Fregia, for their insight and patience—
even when I came late to that ongoing divine
appointment*

❦ and from the three of us to:

*Everyone who sent us their dreams to work with...
we love you.*

1 | INTRODUCTION: BEYOND SLEEP

Only connect! . . . Only connect the prose and the passion, and both will be exalted, and human love will be seen at its height. Live in fragments no longer. . . .

E. M. Forster, *Howard's End*

This workbook and its companion dream journal are both "interactive" and "user-friendly," to borrow now-familiar phrases from the world of computer language. You, the reader, are encouraged to be much more than a mere spectator. This workbook assumes that you will follow the guidelines included in these pages and actually do what is recommended, that you will interact with it. And the dream journal, which is made up almost entirely of empty pages, is absolutely worthless unless you are an active participant in the process described in the workbook. We've made every effort to present the information and the suggestions in a friendly manner, so that you, the user, can easily follow them.

You will not find a lot of dream history here, or even much about the technical side of dreaming. Those aspects of the subject have been extensively covered in many other places, and you are encouraged to search them out and learn more about them (a list of some of these references is provided in Chapter 7 of this workbook). What you *will* find here are clear, step-by-step directions that will show you how to capture, record, organize, and understand your dreams and the immeasurable guidance they have for you.

Eighteen years ago, Pat had an important dream. She was sitting in the driver's seat of a parked car along the side of a road. She saw a woman from whom she had been learning about dream interpretation, Linda, walking down the street towards her. Linda was carrying a small chest. She got in the car with Pat, saying, "I have something for you," and handed her the chest. Pat took the chest, looked inside, and saw an assortment of faceted, unmounted gemstones. She looked at the stones and thought, "These are wonderful and have tremendous value. But I couldn't wear them as they are; I'd have to have them mounted." So Pat said to Linda, "I can't take them." But Linda said, "Yes, you can. They're my legacy to you."

"Linda" is not this woman's real name, but the woman herself was very important in Pat's early learning about dream interpretation. In the dream, Pat has not yet begun to publicly move along her path in the world (she is simply sitting beside the road in a parked car). But Linda is ready to pass along to Pat the ideas, symbols, knowledge, and intuition with which she adorns herself. Pat understands that she will need to alter these parts of Linda's legacy by "mounting" them in her own settings. Then she will be able to "display" the wonderful treasures which Linda is passing on to her.

About This Workbook

This chapter will introduce you to us, the Dream Team, and tell you something about how we came to put this book together. We feel it is important that you know our credentials, since we will be your guides and teachers in what we think should be an important part of anyone's education. Hopefully, knowing something about how we arrived at this point will encourage you as you start along your own path.

We will also tell you something about what is generally understood about dreams and how they work. This is as close as we will come to the historical and technical aspects we mentioned, and it may help you to explain to others why you've suddenly begun to carry your dream journal with you everywhere you go. We have found that more and more people are becoming aware that dreams are trying to tell them something, but there are still a few holdouts who haven't got that message yet and who will ask you why you think your dreams are so important. This section will help you respond to them.

In Chapter 2, we lay out the steps for investigating your dreams and extracting their messages. This chapter stresses the need for using your dream journal, either the one in the back of this workbook or some other notebook that you may prefer, so that you can capture your dreams, connected events, and emotions on paper, and begin to look at them more closely. Chapter 3 will talk about dreams in general, what forms they take, what guidance you can expect to receive from them, and how they are likely to present that guidance to you.

Chapter 4 shows you how to take the information you write down about a dream, apply the general knowledge about how dreams work, and decipher or interpret the dream to find the message and guidance in your dream. There is even a tutorial, which "walks" you through several dreams to show you how to work with the material in your dream journal.

Chapter 5 discusses dream symbols and how they work. It helps you to understand both the broad "universal" meaning that a symbol can have and also the "particular" or personal meaning it has for you. In fact, this chapter shows you how to make your own "living" dictionary of dream symbols, which grows as you add meanings from your own life and dream experiences.

Chapter 6 is sort of an optional chapter. It contains a "dream walk" exercise which we like to do when we give seminars. In addition, there are several short discussions about some unusual aspects of dreaming which may be of interest. Finally, Chapter 7 provides references to other works about dreams and dreaming as we promised. Though this is not by any means a comprehensive list, it includes works we have enjoyed and learned from. We encourage you to investigate these books and tapes—as well as the many other works to which they refer—for more about dreams and dreaming.

The Authors

We are Pat and Jim Fregia (say *Free-jay*), and we have been calling ourselves the Dream Team since about 1987, when we first began to appear on an afternoon talk show on KPRC, a Houston radio station. However, we have both been working with dreams for much longer than that.

Pat began to interpret dreams at a very young age. At first, she concentrated on her own dreams, but then, as her skill grew and her abilities began to be known, friends began to ask her for help. Now she provides guidance in interpretation for both friends and strangers at—literally—any hour of every day.

Both Pat and Jim read voraciously in this field, attend seminars on dreams whenever they are available, and work with a number of people who are themselves skilled in dream interpretation. One of the most important of these was the late Elsie Sechrist, author of *Dreams: Your Magic Mirror*, at the Association for Research and Enlightenment (ARE) in Virginia Beach, and at the Jung Center in Houston.

Jim, a retired Air Force Colonel, is a professor of psychology at Brazosport College, in Lake Jackson, Texas. Before his retirement from the Air Force, he taught at Air University at Maxwell Air Force Base in Montgomery, Alabama. While his work with dreams did not begin as early as Pat's, he, too, has become skilled at understanding and interpreting dreams. In addition, he uses dreams to help his hypnosis and regression patients to pinpoint hidden traumas.

Together, the Fregias founded the OmniCenter, a holistic health center in a community near their home. They have presented seminars on dreams throughout the south and southwest and have published articles in several newspapers and in *Venture Inward*, the monthly magazine of the Association for Research & Enlightenment (A.R.E.).

Pat Bonney Shepherd, the adjunct member of the Dream Team, should be mentioned here: she provides the writing and editorial skills required to bring order to the huge amount of raw material which the Fregias have accumulated after more than fifteen years of working on dreams. In 1983, when she and the Fregias met, she knew almost nothing about dreams or their importance. She has been learning hard and fast since then and can point out where clarification is needed and where material should be omitted as irrelevant or too technical. (However, please note that, when "Pat" is mentioned in the text of the workbook, it is Pat Fregia who is meant.)

There, that's who we are. Now, if this were an ideal world, each of you would introduce yourselves, and we could work on your dreams face to face. To some extent, however, even if we could work individually with each of you, we would not necessarily be able to truly and completely understand what your dream is telling you. That is for you to discover.

The "Great Aha!"

The dream is the royal road to the unconscious.

Sigmund Freud

In fact, we must offer a word of caution here, which you should keep in mind as you work through what we say in the rest of this workbook. **Only you can finally provide the true interpretation and meaning of your dreams.** We are your assistants or co-interpreters: we can tell you how dreams generally work, we can show you how to organize the material that is presented to you in a dream, we can tell you what the images in your dreams generally mean to most people, and we can guide you in finding what those same images probably mean to you specifically.

But only you can work through each dream and reach what we call the great "Aha!" message.

You dreamed the dream; *your* unconscious built it out of *your* life's experiences, understandings, concerns and joys, ideas and memories. The messages of the dream are those which *your* higher consciousness wants you to receive.

The exceptions occur when you consciously don't want to hear what your dreams are telling you. At such times, you are (as Jim, the psychologist part of the team, would say) "in denial." An example Jim encounters often in his counseling sessions involves someone who is receiving a recurring dream, which Jim sees as an urging to quit a bad habit (such as smoking, drinking, or overeating). But the dreamer doesn't want to quit, and so he or she is not ready to "Aha!" that interpretation. In such a case, Jim can only be patient and wait for the dreamer to finally open up to the message.

So as long as you can trust yourself to honestly hear what your dreams are telling you, don't accept anyone else's suggestion or assistance without checking to see if it meets the "Aha!" test: if it just doesn't speak to you, then either you're not ready for the message or it may not be the *right* answer and you must keep looking.

We once worked with a woman, Polly, who was having recurring dreams about being chased by a giant fork and spoon. She was dangerously overweight, but she consciously professed to be happy with herself the way she was. As we worked with her dreams, we found it hard to interpret these eating utensils as symbolizing anything but an obsession with food. But Polly told us repeatedly that this interpretation just didn't seem accurate to her. She wasn't able to come up with an alternative interpretation, though. Our feeling, after a lot of hard work on these dreams, was that Polly was running from the truth. She was just not ready to listen to the message of these dreams.

Other Resources

No one is a light unto himself, not even the Sun.
A. Porchia

Having said that, we must quickly add that there are many places where you can and will find valuable help in understanding what your dreams mean: your best friend, your spouse, your mother, your co-workers or classmates—in short, from those who know you and interact with you in a fairly regular and meaningful way. Those who have shared some part of your life often remind you of events you had forgotten, make connections between ideas or events or people that might not occur to you, or in some other way help you to rearrange the elements of your dream so that, suddenly, there it is: that "Aha!" feeling that tells you that you have found what you needed to see.

In addition, you may be able to find a dream partner or organize a dream support group to help you in interpreting your dreams. When two or more people meet on a fairly regular basis to share dreams and "bounce" ideas off each other, they begin to develop a shared understanding of the way dream symbols work. A dream partner will remember, for example, that two or three of your most recent dreams have taken place in the kitchen. When you then tell the group your latest dream, in which you're buying saucepans in a department store, your partner can make a connection between this latest dream and the other kitchen dreams, a connection that you might not see because you're concentrating on another aspect of the dream.

Be warned, however, that dreams can reveal very personal information about the dreamer. In telling us their dreams, people have sometimes unknowingly revealed more to us than they intended. We do not say this to discourage you from using dream partners or groups but simply to advise you to choose those partners and groups with care.

This workbook provides a way to think about your dreams that can direct you along the most productive life path. A very simple example will clarify this. Most people at one point or another dream about death: someone they know well, someone they've never seen before, or a figure whose face they cannot make out will die in a dream. Does this mean that an actual death will occur in these dreamers' lives? There are rare occasions when that is, in fact, the meaning of the dream. But most of the time such a dream has quite a different meaning.

This workbook will show you how to look at the circumstances surrounding that dreamed death, find the details that will help you to understand it, and pull from all of that data the "Aha!" meaning. We will discuss death as a dream symbol in later chapters; for now, let's just say you will probably find that what has died or is dying is not a person but a relationship, or some habit or trait in your character, or a project or phase in your life. You—and only you—will know what it is as soon as you come upon it. Through the activities and guidance provided in this workbook, we will have shown you how to look at the dream event in such a way that you can see the message it has for you.

Pat and Byrd have been dream partners for nearly twenty-five years now. Byrd has great language skills, a cornball sense of humor, and the ability to provide lots of help for Pat with the puns and sound-alikes that constantly show up in dreams. Pat, on the other hand, can help Byrd by tying together the symbols and pulling up the underlying meanings in Byrd's dreams. Every serious dreamer needs a Byrd in his or her life.

When Byrd moved to a distant city several years ago, the telephone rang off the hook early on many mornings as the two partners worked with each other on the night's "crop" of dreams. Lately, though, Pat has found she can go to Byrd in the middle of a dream and ask her for help with a pun or verbal joke; she usually gets an answer in the dream. Byrd, too, rings Pat's dream telephone quite often for help on her own dream problems. (More on this in Chapter 6.)

So use this workbook, use your friends and family, use your co-workers and colleagues, use all the help that is offered—use it eagerly and happily. But be just as eager and happy to take from it only what speaks to you and toss away the rest. Remember at all times: there is only one person who can tell you what your dreams mean, and that one person is you (unless, of course, you're in heavy-duty denial). Our hope is that, as time goes on, you will need to consult the workbook portion of this book less and less as you become practiced in the techniques it offers. Finally, the only tools you will need will be those you use to record your dreams (your journal and a pen, a pad of paper and a pencil, or even a tape recorder) and your own mental processes.

Some Background Questions: "Why? When? How? . . ."

Why should we study our dreams? It's work, often hard work. Why should we give ourselves one more chore to perform each day? After all, dreams have been ignored for centuries. Most of us in the western world who have had any connection with the Bible can remember some stories involving dreams, but there has been precious little else in the centuries since.

In fact, the Bible includes over seventy references to dreams. Probably the most well-known concerns Joseph, whose brothers sold him into slavery in Egypt where he became the captive of Egypt's pharaoh. One night the pharaoh dreamed that seven fat cows went into the Nile River, and, when they came out, they were seven skinny cows. Joseph had a reputation, even in jail, for his dream interpretation, so the pharaoh sent for him. Joseph heard the dream and told the pharaoh that there would be seven prosperous years for the kingdom, followed by seven years of drought and famine, and that the pharaoh should husband his supplies accordingly. The pharaoh did better than that: he freed Joseph and put him in charge of doing the husbanding. Egypt came through the crisis very well, and Joseph wound up its prime minister.

American Indians believed dreams were a way of communicating with spirits for the purpose of seeking supernatural powers. The mind could be purified through dreams, creativity could be enhanced, and messages from loved ones who went back to the earth could be received from dreams. Dreams of animals contained the most power. For an Oglala Indian, a buffalo dream would bring strength. To a Crow, a dream of the sun (the Chief of the sky beings) meant a short life, while a dream about the moon offered a long life.

Because dreams were so powerful, it was important to be able to "catch" dreams. Many Native American tribes used "dream catchers" at the entrance to their teepees. These were always made in the shape of a circle or "hoop," signifying wholeness. A drawing of a dream catcher is presented as the frontispiece of this book. For Indians, wholeness is wisdom based not on the duration of life, but rather on the fullness with which each being enters each moment. The dream catcher helped one along the path to wholeness because it caused the bad dreams and spirits to be caught in the web at the center of the dream catcher, while the good dreams, bringing supernatural powers and guidance, would flow through to the dreamer.

There are more references to dreams in the New Testament. We read there of another Joseph, Mary's husband, who was warned in a dream that his family was in danger. He heeded that dream and fled to Egypt, thereby saving the baby Jesus from certain death at the hands of Herod's men.

But those dreams were dreamed many years ago. Today, much of the world would be shocked if they heard that the president of the United States, or Britain's prime minister, or a leader of any one of the former Soviet republics woke up each morning and called for coffee, the morning papers—and the Chief Dream Interpreter! In the centuries that followed the birth of Christ and that culminated in the so-called Age of Reason, in which scientific method and quantifiable measurement were the only valid means of evaluating the human experience, dreams and other such metaphysical events began to be seen as suspicious, evil, even the work of the devil. By Shakespeare's time, dreams were not always considered evil, but they had certainly lost the status they once had for both of the Josephs. Here's what we read in *Romeo and Juliet:*

> *True, I talk of dreams;*
> *Which are the children of an idle brain,*
> *Begot of nothing but of vain fantasy;*
> *Which is as thin of substance as the air,*
> *And more inconstant than the wind…*

From Freud to Jung—and Beyond

The conscious mind allows itself to be trained like a parrot, but the unconscious does not—which is why St. Augustine thanked God for not making him responsible for his dreams.

Carl Jung, *Psychology and Alchemy*

Sigmund Freud re-awakened our interest in dreams. Freud's important contribution to the field of dreams was his explanation that dreams bring messages from the unconscious mind. Psychoanalysis, based on Freudian concepts, operates on the premise that any person's problems are the result of psychological trauma from the past, which has been repressed and kept in the unconscious. We need to bring this repressed material to the conscious mind, say psychoanalysts, where we can remember it and deal with it. Freud, and those who followed him, felt that dreams served as the primary channel for getting information from the unconscious to the conscious.

Freud went even further and decided that virtually every dream released and gave expression to a wish which the dreamer had to either control or suppress in his or her waking life. Because Freud worked during Victorian times when sexual repression was the norm, most of his patients told him of dreams in which sexual themes were prominent. He naturally concluded from these findings that dreams were always sexual in nature. Of course, one hundred years later, in much less repressive times, people still do have sexual dreams; we frequently hear dreams from people that sound like those analyzed by Freud. And while his basic premise that dreams carry messages from the unconscious is very useful, those working in the field have moved away from a primarily sexual focus in dream interpretation.

But Freud's ideas helped to shed light on another important question: if dreams are simply telling us about material we have repressed in our unconscious, why don't they clearly elucidate that which is repressed? Why are our dreams so often confused, illogical, and seemingly meaningless?

Freud said that dreams bring our repressed wishes to the surface; but, as those dreams are brought up from the unconscious, they must still get past the mental police constantly on duty to keep us from suffering too much anxiety. When we are awake, that force is strong and effective; during sleep, it is somewhat relaxed and weaker, but it is still there. For this reason, Freud felt, the unconscious masks its messages, even censors them. Thus, our dreams reflect our wishes, but they have been disguised after their journey through this censoring mechanism, and they come to us in symbolic form.

Freud's most famous disciple was Carl Jung, and it was Jung who really worked out a viable dream theory. He decided that some of the symbols appearing in dreams have a universal quality to them. By that, Jung meant that, because of their physical qualities or utility, these symbols evoke the same kinds of responses regardless of the culture or the experiences of the dreamer. For example, a tree is seen as a source of life and protection in most cultures, whether the tree is a date-bearing palm in the tropics or a tall sheltering pine in the north country. A vehicle of any sort carries us on our life's journey, whether that vehicle is a wagon, a car, a boat, or a plane. Jung was able to discuss and define a large number of these symbols, thus providing a substantial foundation in universal dream symbology. Of course objects in dreams have individual meanings for each of us, but Jung's concept of universal dream symbols is solid, valuable, helpful, and has stood the test of time.

There's an interesting story that comes from the early days of this country which provides a vivid example of the power and, well, universality of universal symbols. It seems that Ben Franklin was one of several who wanted to choose a symbol for the colonies, a sort of rallying image with which the colonists could identify and which would help them to work together in the difficult times they faced. His first choice for this symbol was the turkey, for a number of very sensible reasons, such as its wiliness and its great importance as a source of food during the country's earliest times.

But too many others saw the turkey as undignified at best, and downright ugly and stupid at worst. In the end, Franklin had to give in, and the eagle, which stood in most people's minds for independence and majesty, was substituted as the symbol for our young nation.

Interestingly, a number of European countries use the eagle as a national symbol on their flags, proving that people everywhere see it as an inspiring and representative image for their nation. However, after considerable research, we have not yet found one country which has chosen the turkey for this important job.

The "Science" of Dreams

The next major step in dream interpretation came in 1952, when experimenters became aware of the phenomenon known as rapid eye movement (REM). During sleep, rapid eye movement signals that a subject follows objects in a dream with eye movements. This discovery has opened the way for sleep research now being carried out in more than twenty universities in this country alone. There are still many unanswered questions and much to be learned about interpreting dreams, but it's an active, exciting, and important field which continues to gain more and more attention.

Researchers now know that when we sleep, we go through cycles, each involving four types of sleep. These stages are easily distinguished by the patterns of brain activity, which are recorded in electro-encephalograms (EEGs). Each stage is deeper than the one before; at the end of the fourth and deepest stage of sleep, eighty to ninety minutes after having fallen asleep, the sleeper returns quickly to the first stage, and the cycle is repeated.

Observers had long noted that a sleeper's eyes moved rapidly under closed lids at certain times of the night. Research showed that, if awakened during these periods of rapid eye movement, the sleeper would invariably be dreaming. Once EEG technology was available, it was soon clear this REM activity occurred during the first stage of the sleep cycle. The first stage of the first cycle does not usually include dreams; dreaming begins during the first stage of the second cycle of sleep. REM at this point lasts perhaps ten minutes; in later cycles, the REM stage lasts longer and the deeper sleep stages are over more quickly or are not reached at all.

During a normal eight-hour night, most of us will go through the sleep cycle four or five times, with at least one dream during each cycle after the initial one. Usually the first dream of the night will be a sort of "video-taped" replay of an important event of the day just ended. But the dream will often twist this replay around so that the events in the dream come out more to our liking. For example, if, during the day, the dreamer had a confrontation with someone and was the loser in the encounter, in the replay, the dreamer might be the winner. This opening dream provides a sort of theme which will reappear in some form in later dream cycles during the night.

Each dream takes us deeper into the unconscious, and some dreamers can remember three or four dreams each night. Most of us, though, remember only the latest dream, which is also the one from deepest in our unconscious. Thus, the dreamer dreaming of a confrontation might find help in a dream on how to handle a similar confrontation the next time it occurs, how to avoid it, or how to look at it differently and move beyond it. But count on it: there is help from the unconscious if we look for it and work at understanding it.

There is no such thing as a useless dream; dreams have a purpose. Yet with our sleep pattern following this cyclical format, what we remember is rather like

1 4

the last act of a five-act play. What went on before? Is it important in understanding what we *can* remember? Or can we learn enough from that last act to benefit from it?

One of the best ways to answer these questions is to notice the connection between what happened yesterday and the important problems we are currently dealing with in our lives. If we can work backwards through our dream with that in mind, interpreting the various symbols, then we can begin to make more sense out of this final act we're left with each morning. We will discuss this further in Chapter 2.

Let's return to our discussion about what we are coming to know about dreams and dreaming on the scientific front. Dream research shows that 1) we *all* dream every night; 2) dreams occur approximately every ninety minutes; 3) everyone has four or five dreams per night and 4) we all *need* to dream regularly. It has become clear through studies involving sleep deprivation that, when we don't dream regularly, it isn't long before we find ourselves in some sort of psychological trouble.

Other studies have shown that drugs are a major inhibitor of dreams. For example, it is now suspected that *delirium tremens* (d.t.'s), which alcoholics suffer from, occur because the drinker's dreams have been blocked by the alcohol. The dreams accumulate and, rather than occurring during sleep, come in this waking state after an extensive period of time passes without dreaming. The same is true with drugs such as barbiturates. It is felt that the addiction to such drugs is in part caused by the drug-taker's terror at the nightmares that occur when the drug is discontinued.

Here's an interesting tidbit: at one time, it was thought that dreams lasted only a fraction of a second. There are many people who still believe this. The theory was proposed in the early 1860s by a Frenchman, André Maury, who was a writer and a monarchist at an inconvenient time. Obviously worried for his own safety, one night he dreamed that he was arrested, tried, and guillotined. Maury realized, when he woke up, that the bed had broken and part of the bed frame had hit him on the back of the neck. He deduced from this that the whole dream had to have occurred during the brief moment between the time the bed broke and the time he felt the impact on his neck. How else, he reasoned, would he have been prepared in the dream for the sensation? Others accepted his theory, and thus it was believed for decades that dreams were very brief.

However, once the research on dreaming really began in earnest, and especially after researchers were aware of REM sleep and what it signified, it became clear that dreams can last from two minutes to an hour. Most dreams last from fifteen to twenty minutes. Because the unconscious is an extremely efficient playwright, in the few seconds it takes for a stimulus such as an alarm, the ringing of a phone, or the smell of coffee brewing to reach our conscious minds, the unconscious has often found a way to incorporate it into the dream we are having at that time.

With this modern understanding, we can see that perhaps Mr. Maury's unconscious, in his dream of arrest and trial, might originally have been planning on life imprisonment or death by firing squad; when the bed frame hit him on the back of the neck, however, the efficient scriptwriter quickly changed the dream's outcome.

Questions? . . .

As soon as you trust yourself, you will know how to live.
Johann W. Von Goethe

When we give our seminars, we find that, once people are aware of the importance of dreams for all aspects of their lives, there are a number of questions which always seem to come up. Let's look at a few of these:

Q: *When I'm awake, I think logically, but my dreams don't seem so logical. Why is that?*

One of the characteristics of the dream state is that it frees our logical mind. We dream that we are doing all kinds of physical things—running, flying, swimming —some of which we don't consider ourselves capable of doing when we're conscious, and none of which we are actually doing as we are dreaming. During a dream, our mind/body sort of shifts into neutral, and our thoughts are less restrained. The rules of good/normal/logical behavior are suspended. So it becomes logical that our dreams are not themselves logical. As Freud noted, this could be considered one of the main purposes of dreaming.

In dreams we often act out frustrations, anger, hostilities. We've been raised to be polite and restrained in our actions, and so we hide these things from others and even from ourselves. In a dream, all this politeness and restraint can be put aside. If we don't like someone, we can chop them up into little pieces in a dream and flush them down the toilet. Marlene's dream above is a good example of how this can be done.

Being able to do this without repercussions helps us in at least two ways: first, we are able to release some pent-up anger in a non-threatening way, and second, we may be getting a message from our unconscious that we don't like someone whom we may have been telling ourselves in our waking state that we do like. Both purposes are possible.

Now, we need to point out that not all dreams are as wild and crazy as this. In fact, some people dream rather straightforward dreams most of the time. Jim's usual mode of thought is matter-of-fact—left-brained, to use today's psychological jargon—and, although he has his share of "illogically" symbolic dreams, his dreams often have a matter-of-fact directness to them. Pat, on the other hand, is more right-brained and thinks in images and emotional nuances. Her dreams tend to take her normally vivid imagery and "run with it."

Marlene has dreams of stuffing dead bodies into a vent-hole under the floor in her house. The hole fills up, and the bodies begin to overflow. She pushes them down, trying to hide them.

The message from her subconscious is clear. She is repressing a great many old frustrations and angers and resentments, stuffing them deep into her unconscious. But she has finally reached the point where the process has to stop, where these resentments have begun to overflow, to erupt out of her unconscious. Her conscious mind just can't push them down to repress them anymore.

To illustrate what we mean by matter-of-fact dreams, here's one that Jim had several years ago when he was venturing into the commodities market. As Jim tells it: "I dreamed, one night, that I was on the floor of the Chicago commodities market (where, in fact, I've never been). There was a mass of paper strewn all over the floor. I reached down and picked up one of the pieces of paper. At the top, it said "Wheat," and there were figures in a column below that word, 575, then 525, then 400, and so on, all the way down the page.

"I woke up, thought about the dream for a while, then called my broker and told him to buy four contracts in wheat to go down, because that's the way the figures went. I held on to those contracts for three months and sold them when they had arrived at the figure at the bottom of the list I had seen in my dream. I made $10,000 on that transaction. Now, I could have held on to the contracts and might have made more money if I had. But the dream only showed a certain figure, and I felt that I should follow that lead."

Q: *Often when I have a physically active dream, I wake up exhausted, as if I had been undergoing whatever intense activity I dreamed about. Why is this?*

This happens because your muscles may in fact be physiologically responding to the dream activity. This is what happens when dogs or other animals sleep and we see their legs moving jerkily and hear them make soft noises. Normally, a mechanism in the brain kicks in when we sleep to inhibit this activity, but there are times (as, for example, in sleep-walking) when this mechanism doesn't work quite as effectively as it should.

Q: *I feel like I need eight hours of sleep, but I don't get that during the week, and I can rarely remember my dreams. But on the weekends when I can sleep more, I do remember my dreams much more consistently.*

As you'll see in the next chapter, this is to be expected. But it is also valid from a scientific point of view. As we said, dreams come during the first phase of the sleep cycle. If we are awakened before we reach that point in the cycle, it may have been sixty to seventy minutes since our last dream, which will make it much harder for us to remember that previous dream. On the other hand, if we sleep for a normal amount of time and wake up naturally, as many of us can do on weekends, we will probably have just finished a dream, and it will still be fresh and vivid in our minds.

Again, Pat and Jim can serve as examples: Jim generally wakes up early each morning and gets out of bed right away to begin his morning routine. In contrast, Pat lies in bed for a while and takes the time to review what she was dreaming. Probably for this reason, Pat can remember many more dreams than Jim can. As you will see when we talk about dream recall, some people find that setting the alarm to give themselves a few extra minutes to lie quietly and review their dreams serves as a wonderful help in remembering those dreams.

Q: In the past, my dreams were always stressful. These days, though, they're much more pleasant. What's happening?

That depends on what's going on in your life. Dreams almost always focus on the most important event or events occurring in your life right now. Your dreams are not imagined plots from some unconscious soap opera: they are related to what's going on in your life as you live it.

We once worked with a woman who had experienced a recurring dream for a number of years. It involved soldiers fighting a civil war in a big southern mansion. The dream turned out to be a warning to her of a problem with her blood (this is what we have labeled a physical dream, and we discuss it in more detail in Chapter 3). She told us that she had often been anemic throughout her life, and we felt that she probably had this dream at the onset of each of her bouts of anemia. We also suggested that, shortly before she had this dream for the first time, she had seen a movie or read a book that dealt with the Civil War and the South (possibly *Gone With the Wind*). These images must have been vivid in her mind, and so the unconscious used them as building blocks for the message it needed to convey.

But if this woman had been caught up with, say, the civil strife in Northern Ireland, the unconscious could just as easily have used that setting for the message. What we need to understand is that the unconscious is very resourceful and uses the material that has made a conscious impact on us during the day or at some point in our recent past as the web on which the particular message of a given dream is woven.

To Sum Up

Let's summarize what we've covered so far. We've talked a bit about how people in Western cultures have looked at dreams and dreaming, about the kinds of things we now know about dreams and sleep, and about what we might be able to learn from our dreams. But we need to stress here, as we will throughout the discussion which follows, that though there are some things that are generally true about all dreams and dreamers, for each individual dreamer the dream patterns and the way in which dreams present their material will be unique. In this workbook, we can present techniques and suggestions to help each of you as you examine your dreams, but that's all we can do. Most of the work of actual interpretation must be done by you, the dreamer. Your dream, after all, has a message which is almost always intended only for you. So it follows that only you can experience that great "Aha!" feeling as you discover the key to the meaning of a dream.

With that in mind, let's move on to Chapter 2, where we will talk about some of the very practical things you can do to prepare yourself and your unconscious mind to remember, recall, understand, and interpret your dreams. You may begin by asking your unconscious these questions:

1) What would you have me hear?

2) What would you have me see?

3) What would you have me do?

2 | THE THREE "Rs" OF DREAMING: KEEPING A DREAM JOURNAL

You cannot be totally committed sometimes.

Textbook, *A Course in Miracles*

One of the most important steps in becoming your own best dream interpreter is learning to record your dreams. You may already have been doing this in some fashion, and if so, you're well along the path to dream analysis. But let's assume for now that you either have never recorded your dreams or have only done the job occasionally—just a note now and then on a scrap of paper that happened to be handy as you woke up after a particularly strange or vivid dream.

As you may suspect, there is a better way, one that will not only provide you with a record of your dreams but that can help you to understand what they mean. In this section of the workbook, you will find some practical procedures to follow before you dream and after you wake up, to encourage you to remember what you have dreamed. In addition, this section will show you how to write down your dreams in a dream journal (such as the one which makes up the last section of this book) or on a simple pad of paper, if that's what you prefer. You will see how to examine your dreams and extract their essential information, what additional information from outside of the dream should be noted, and how to write all of this information down and organize it so that it will be most helpful to you.

If you have never—or hardly ever—kept any kind of a dream journal, and even if you have faithfully and completely recorded every dream you've ever had, read on to find out how you can sharpen your skills and develop your own inborn talents to guide yourself by using your own dreams.

Preparations Before Dreaming

You can actually prepare yourself to remember your dreams. Most people either don't realize this or don't accept it as true, but there are several steps that you can follow before you go to sleep that will increase the chances of remembering what you dream.

We are *not* saying here that these preparations will help you to dream. This, of course, is because you already *do* dream—we all do, several times every night, as we explained in Chapter 1. Rather, these preparations will help you become more and more *conscious* of your unconscious dream activity. And, if you already remember your dreams, one or more each night, following the routine we will describe will help you to become even better at this task.

We are going to suggest several steps for this purpose. Some of these steps involve physical activities, others involve mental activities. If you pick those which seem right for you and then follow them consistently and habitually, you will strengthen your dream memory "muscles." The same principle is at work here as in any other field of endeavor: whether you want to learn to play the piano, to do calligraphy, to run Olympic races, or to be more organized, constant practice is necessary to strengthen the mental or physical muscles involved in the activity. At the very least, performing some or all of the steps suggested here will help you to focus your waking mind on dreams, and the more often you can bring your mind to focus on something, the stronger its force becomes in your life.

Physical Preparation

Let's look first at what can be done on the physical level. As a foundation for this dream memory routine, we recommend that you consider taking Vitamin B6, especially if you seldom or never remember your dreams. Dr. Lendon Smith, in his book *Feed Yourself Right*, explains that this vitamin has properties that increase circulation, and it has been shown that, when Vitamin B6 intake is increased and circulation increases, dream memory increases. The amount to take varies; Dr. Smith suggests that you gradually increase your intake until you find yourself beginning to remember dreams. However, vitamins, when taken in high doses, may be toxic to your system. Check with your doctor or your local pharmacy for safe levels of vitamin intake.

Basic health measures can only help you in remembering your dreams. Drink lots of water (six to eight glasses per day). Be sure to excercise consistently. Any type of aerobic activity for twenty minutes three times during the week will increase overall well-being and health; and, very important for our purposes, exercise helps you sleep more soundly. (Be sure to do strenuous excercise no later than three hours before bedtime). Try to keep a very consistent sleep schedule. Go to bed at the same time each night, get as much sleep as your particular body needs, and arise at the same time each morning. This routine is very beneficial for sound sleep and dream memory. Also, you may try some form of meditation for relaxation and mental/physical clarity. Check your local library for books on the subject of meditation. Finally, it is important to eat a balanced diet, full of vitamins and nutrients, to help keep you lucid and strong on your new dream journey. However, try not to eat anything three hours before retiring to bed. If you must, be sure it is a light snack.

Establishing a routine to be followed as conscientiously as possible every night before we go to bed will do a great deal to encourage an open unconscious. The particular steps we follow are generally not as important as our faithfulness in following those steps. A little farther along, we will suggest a number of activities you can try. Choose the ones that fit your lifestyle; discard those that don't. Then follow the routine you have chosen as faithfully as you can for a period of at least three weeks. (Three weeks has been shown to be the minimal length of time required to develop—or change—a habit.)

Mental Preparation

The Wright brothers flew right through
the smokescreen of impossibility.

Charles F. Kettering

To provide the proper emotional foundation, it is very important to keep a positive attitude toward the whole process. Dreams have their source in the unconscious, and each of us can help "program" our unconscious to behave as we wish it to. This is a tool few of us realize we possess.

"Programming," as we use the term here, means convincing our unconscious that we *want* to become aware of our dreams, that we are ready to receive information, and that we intend to use that information and the guidance it can provide in our daily lives. Remember, our unconscious is always aware, always listening to us and absorbing everything we experience. If we flippantly say, "Oh, I never can remember my dreams," our unconscious (which does not deal in emotion) hears this only as an instruction, a "negative affirmation," if you will. As a result, we won't remember our dreams. On the other hand, if we begin to send instructions, often and consistently and on all levels, that we want to remember our dreams, then our unconscious hears and responds.

Try to counter any tendency you might have to be discouraged or discouraging about dream retention, as it's called. Stop yourself before you make a negative remark about your efforts. As Thumper says in the Disney classic, *Bambi*, "If you can't say sumfin' nice, don't say nuffin' at all." If you speak to your friends or your family on the subject, say things like, "I'm really working hard to try to remember what I dream." And write your goals down. When you put objectives in clear black and white, your unconscious receives this reinforcing information and will be even more likely to take you seriously.

What are some of the goals that might inspire you to work at dream retention? They will vary, of course, from dreamer to dreamer, but most will focus on developing, broadening, and encouraging the help and assistance available from your higher consciousness—that "still, small voice" that is often so hard to hear in today's noisy, busy world.

As we work through relationships with family or friends, situations at work or at home, we seek constantly to understand these encounters and situations so that we can improve them. We read books, we listen to tapes, we ask others for help, we seek out professionals, we worry and turn the problem over and over in our conscious minds. In almost every case, some of the most valuable help we can receive is there for the taking in our dreams each night. By tuning in to the messages available in dreams, we can literally discover what we really think about a situation or a relationship.

We might also see our dreams as providing a source of creative ideas, as they have for so many imaginative people throughout history. Below are some well-known ideas that came in "night-time postcards" to authors, artists, scientists and engineers.

"Literary works that have been directly inspired by dreams include Robert Louis Stevenson's The Strange Case of Dr. Jekyll and Mr. Hyde, *Francis Thompson's* 'The Hound of Heaven,' *DeQuincey's* Confessions of an Opium Eater, *and Bunyan's* Pilgrim's Progress. *Coleridge composed* 'Kubla Khan' *largely in a dream, Voltaire dreamed a whole canto of* 'La Henriade', *and Thackeray got the title* 'Vanity Fair' *from a dream. . . .*

"The 'closed-chain' theory of Friedrich August Kekulé, which revolutionized the study of chemistry, was revealed to the great chemist in a dream. Kekulé dreamed of dancing atoms taking on the shape of a snake which then swallowed its own tail and began whirling. This image led to Kekulé's discovery that benzene has a ringlike structure, which in turn demonstrated the importance of molecular structure in organic chemistry. . . .

"Inventor Elias Howe perfected a contraption for making clothes thanks to a dream. In the dream he was captured by spear-carrying savages, who were about to execute him for his failure to produce a

workable machine when he noticed that their spears all had eye-shaped holes near the tips. He woke up, rushed to his lab, moved the hole in his needle down near the point, and the sewing machine had been invented...."

Anonymous, Dream Diary

Take some time to sit quietly and determine what specific issues you would like to receive help on or where some additional creative input would be helpful (both Pat Fregia and Pat Shepherd went to sleep many a night during the course of writing this book with very specific requests for dream assistance). Then write down these specific ideas. These written statements, coupled with positive statements spoken aloud, provide evidence that you are serious.

In case it seems that we are going a bit overboard with these suggestions for communicating your intentions to the unconscious, let us make a point here. Exaggeration is a tool that the unconscious uses and understands. Proof of this shows up every night in our dreams. So use this tool yourself: Repeat as often as you can, "I will remember my dreams." Post large reinforcing messages where you can see them throughout the day. Write down your goals and objectives and review them everyday. In other words, be very deliberate and focused as you follow your dream retention routine, at least for the first few weeks.

Most importantly, keep a positive attitude about the whole endeavor. Remember, for years you've been ignoring the messages and guidance which have been available in your dreams. It's as if you've received a special delivery letter marked "Personal" each morning, but you've tossed it on the table unopened. Your first job every morning should be to eagerly open that letter and, with great anticipation, try to understand what it tells you. Use all the skills and craft of Sherlock Holmes, if necessary, until the meaning is clear. Once you begin to do this, you will be replacing the old message you've been sending to your unconscious with a strong new message: "Hey, I'm really serious. I know you've got a message for me, and I promise to pay attention."

Chris Stevens, one of the unique characters on the television program "Northern Exposure," said in a recent episode:

"Dreams are postcards from the subconscious, inner self to outer self, right brain trying to cross that moat to the left. All too often they come back unread, 'Return to Sender, Address Unknown.' That's a shame, too, because there's a whole different world out there—or in here, depending on your point of view.

"Indeed, for all we know, this very moment could be nothing more than vapors of our own imagination. As Bertrand Russell mused, 'I do not believe that I am now dreaming, but I cannot prove that I am not.' The point being there's more to these nocturnal journeys than has previously been considered or accepted." [CBS TV, November 11, 1991.]

Edgar Cayce read his nightly postcards—and was often at his unconscious mailbox at other times of the day, too. He was known as "the Sleeping Prophet" because of his ability to go at will into a deep trance-like state and give accurate diagnoses with courses of treatment for people whom he did not even have to meet—though he himself had no medical training. He gave over 14,000 of these "readings" for more than 6,000 people. Although he believed very strongly each individual should carefully study his or her own dreams, the information and the technique that became clear through the study of his readings has become widely known and is often used to help in dream interpretation.

"Let us learn to dream, gentlemen, and then
we may perhaps find the truth."
F. A. Kekulé

So you can help yourself physically with doses of Vitamin B6 and emotionally with doses—even over-doses—of positive statements and actions that will convince your unconscious that you are very serious. Now, as you establish this supportive physical and emotional climate, what are some of the specific steps you can routinely take each night before you go to sleep to help remember your dreams?

Be prepared to record your dreams. Depending on what works for you, keep a pencil or pen, your journal or a pad of paper, or a tape recorder beside your bed so that, as soon as you wake up, you can record your dreams and the date they occurred with as little physical disturbance as possible.

This is one of the most basic yet most frequently ignored steps in becoming tuned in to your dreams. However, it is vital for one simple reason: human beings forget things. As the noted dream researcher, Dr. Ann Faraday, has said, "Procrastination is the thief of dreams." We intend to write down our dreams, but we'll do it later, when we have more time. But when later comes and we're ready to write, there's nothing left of the dream but a few rags and tatters.

The late Elsie Sechrist, who worked with Edgar Cayce on dreams and for many years after his death lectured and taught about dreams all over the world, told of the night she woke up after a dream, stumbled to the bathroom, did her business, and then, before going back to bed, picked up a lipstick and wrote a single word in large letters across the mirror. In the morning, her husband was quite taken aback to find red letters across his face as he prepared to shave—but the one word served as a very effective trigger for Elsie, and she was able to completely reconstruct the dream (which otherwise might well have been lost).

Write a memo to your unconscious. Perhaps you have a question for which you'd like an answer. Such a question could be as simple as "Is this the right time to start a diet?" Or it might be as monumental as "Should I buy this business?" (see Chapter 4, p. 82, for a dream received in answer to just that question) or "Why am I so unhappy?" (a dream which responded to this question can be found in Chapter 3, p. 44) Perhaps you'd like an especially peaceful dream to relieve stress after a particularly trying day. Or you might simply state that you wish to remember what you dream.

Whatever your request, write it on a slip of paper. Crumple the piece of paper and place it between the pillowcase and the pillow directly under your head. You will then sleep, but your unconscious will be reminded by both sound and feel all night long of the note and its contents. And we assure you: your question will be addressed in a dream—probably in more than one dream—during the night, though we cannot assure you that you will always understand the response immediately.

Review the previous day's activities or dream journal work. It can be helpful to take a few minutes before turning out the light to empty your mind of the day's stresses and anxieties (or even of the excitement of prime-time TV and/or the late-night news). In addition, this helps to "prime the pump" by replacing such active thoughts with calmer ones. At this time, you could review your previous night's dream, work in your dream journal, or re-read and focus on the goals and objectives you have established for wanting to interpret your dreams. Any one of these activities will help to push distractions out of your mind and "clear the decks" for tonight's show.

As an alternative, you might turn your attention to an event of the day just past for which you have requested clarification in your "pillow note." Going over the event in a calm way can provide a kind of canvas upon which your unconscious can work during the night.

Pat's "wind-down" routine is unvarying: every night, she takes a bath or a hot tub. After a fifteen- or twenty-minute soak, she brushes her teeth, gives her face one more wash, gets a glass of water, puts it beside the bed next to her journal, and then gets into bed. At this point, Jim may be watching the last few minutes of the news. But it is important for Pat that the last thing she watches each night be something light, upbeat, and relatively inconsequential, so when the news is over, she turns to a sit-com of her choosing.

The final step for her, when the lights are out, is to go over her day from beginning to end, pointing out to herself where she could have done better as well as where she was successful (a procedure which is a carry-over from the "examination of conscience" instilled by her early parochial school training). This process does help her the next day, because she can more easily recall the actual events that the unconscious may have used in its nightly dream scenario.

Remember, exaggeration and repetition are
your best friends in these efforts:

I will remember my dreams . . .

I will remember my dreams . . .

I will remember my dreams . . .

I will remember my dreams . . .

I will remember my dreams . . .

I will remember my dreams . . .

I will remember my dreams . . .

I will remember my dreams . . .

I will remember my dreams . . .

I will remember my dreams . . .

Thank you . . .

Be nice to your unconscious—it's a true friend.

Drink water. Funny as it may sound, this is a very effective step. Jim has found that, since what goes in has to come out, an extra glass of water helps him to wake up briefly once or twice during the night for a trip to the bathroom. This allows him to exercise the dream memory muscles (remember, we said he was the logical matter-of-fact member of the team). Because the "wake-up" call comes from an internal source, it will more than likely occur between cycles and therefore soon after a dream. So, before falling back to sleep, don't forget to write down at least a note or two about that dream to help you remember it more fully in the morning.

Remember Pat's bedside glass of water? She finds that, when she wakens in a sort of limbo state, half in and half out of sleep, if she takes a small sip of water, she is awakened just enough to jot down a word or two about a dream, which allows her to recall it in the morning. Thus, using this technique, she is able to remember not only the final "act" of that four- or five-act nightly play, but also some of the preceding acts.

Use pre-sleep suggestion. Once you have turned out the light and are on the verge of falling asleep, try to issue some very clear conscious directives to your unconscious. Decide what you would like to accomplish, state it briefly, and repeat it to yourself three times. For example, you might simply say, "I will remember my dreams." Or, "My dream will help me understand [name the problem you've written as your pillow message or some other topic that concerns you]." Or perhaps, if you are going back to sleep after a trip to the bathroom, you might say, "I will resume dreaming where I left off." This is another technique which has been successful in increasing the power of the mind and one of several which allow you to control your dreaming and which you may want to learn as you progress. We'll talk more about these techniques in Chapters 3 and 4.

Conduct an "REM watch." A technique for "catching" dreams in dream research laboratories is to note when a subject has been in the REM sleep stage for a while. At that point, the sleeper is awakened and can almost always remember a dream. This technique, though somewhat inconvenient, could be applied in your own life. Have a partner watch you to determine when you are in the REM sleep stage. This is usually easy to discover because a sleeper's eyes will move under his or her eyelids at that time. After several minutes of REM eye movement, have your partner wake you up—and be ready to record what you were just dreaming.

After Awakening

The essence of discovery is the unlikely marriage
of previously unrelated things, and the
ultimate matchmaker is the unconscious.

A. Koestler, *The Art of Creation*

There are only three basic steps to follow when you wake up, but they are each extremely important. These might be called the three "Rs" of dreaming for they are probably the most basic techniques which you can use.

Step 1. Rest. As you wake up, try not to move for a few minutes. Dreams are best recalled while your body is still in equilibrium, before you begin moving around. This sounds easy but is often a difficult task. Those who are instantly clear-headed and ready to leap out of bed must restrain themselves and work at remaining still for a few minutes. On the other hand, those who doze in and out of sleep until the very last possible minute must work at gaining consciousness soon enough to allow quiet time for dream work.

The alarm clock may cause a problem here. Its purpose is to jolt us awake—exactly the opposite of what we need to do if we want to remember our dreams. Clearly, using an alarm clock is a serious handicap as our unconscious becomes accessible to us. On the other hand, many of us believe that we'd have a real handicap in our waking lives if we didn't use an alarm clock. The solution is to learn to mentally program each night the time you wish to awaken—don't worry, you will wake up at that time. Jim and Pat have not used an alarm clock for any reason for more than twenty years. You may not be conscious of your unconscious, but your unconscious is always conscious; make it aware of your needs and it will be there for you.

Step 2. Review. It is usually not too difficult, if you have followed Step 1, to remember the end of your dream as you wake up. Step 2 involves reliving the dream, and for some of us, that might mean moving backwards through the events of the dream, saying, "This happened, and before that, this, and before that, this," and so on. This should be a relatively detached session, one in which your conscious mind is simply a bystander, watching as the events of the dream replay themselves. It's very important to grab just a word or two and fix it in your mind—if you don't, it may be gone by the time you get back from the bathroom.

Pat is willing to subject herself to a certain amount of ridicule here and mention that she often reinforces the spirit of this step by walking backwards to the bathroom in the morning. This symbolic action helps her to literally "retrace the steps" of her dream.

Step 3. Record. No matter how good our intentions are or how experienced we are in dream work, we cannot be counted on to remember our dreams. But that is only one reason it is important to write them down. In addition, we can use the written record to provide a sort of timeline or growth chart. Comparing last night's dream with dreams from last week, last year, or ten years ago can help us measure our growth, both in understanding our dreams and in managing our lives. A record of our dreams can also be helpful in showing us patterns or recurring dreams; such information aids us in understanding their significance, as we shall see.

While writing down a complete and detailed version of the dream is the ideal, it is not often practical, especially for those who must obey the clock. We have designed the journal pages to help you quickly jot down the most vital points about your dreams. Such a record may provide enough clues to allow you to fill in missing details later during day or in the evening before you go to bed.

But sometimes there will seem to be no time for even such brief notes. The trick then is to jot down just a key word or symbol: "twins," or "black rose," or "mansion," or "Uncle Henry's plaid coat," or whatever seems most memorable as you move past your ever-ready pad and pencil. When you come back to the dream to flesh it out, one written clue will be many times more reliable than a mental promise to yourself that you will remember later when you "have more time..." (Remember Elsie Sechrist's lipstick on the mirror.)

And what about those times—and there will be many, at least at first—when, in spite of all your efforts, you wake up "dreamless"? Our advice is to follow the three "wake-up" steps we've described anyway, just as if you had remembered a dream:

Rest quietly while you explore the corners of your mind, checking just to be sure there isn't a flutter of color, a wisp of an idea still floating around in there.

Review how you felt as you awakened. Did you feel anxious? Were you smiling to yourself for some unexplained reason? Were you sad? Even if these feelings don't help you to remember the actual dream, they can be used cumulatively to help you refine your insight into your general state. And be sure to write down in your journal how you felt when you woke up. Even when you don't remember a dream, your waking emotion could provide an answer to a "pillow talk" question. A general sense of unhappiness or uneasiness as you wake up is a fairly strong signal that the answer to your question is "No," while a happy, contented feeling is probably a signal to "go for it."

Record something in your journal, whether you remember your dream or not. Note, for example, that you asked such-and-such a question before going to sleep, and that you didn't remember a dream, but that you woke with such-and-such a feeling. In this way, you provide more evidence for your unconscious that you are truly serious in this undertaking; you reinforce the habit you are consciously trying to learn; and you create a record to which you can refer later. Won't it be great when you notice after a time that you've moved from remembering one dream per month to more than one per week?

Most importantly, continue to speak positively to yourself about your quest. Don't let discouragement show in your attitude because it will surely be detected by the ever-conscious unconscious. "Productive sleeping can be yours," says Pat. After all, she notes, "I do my best and most creative work when I'm asleep."

I sleep and my heart wakes.
Richard Rolfe

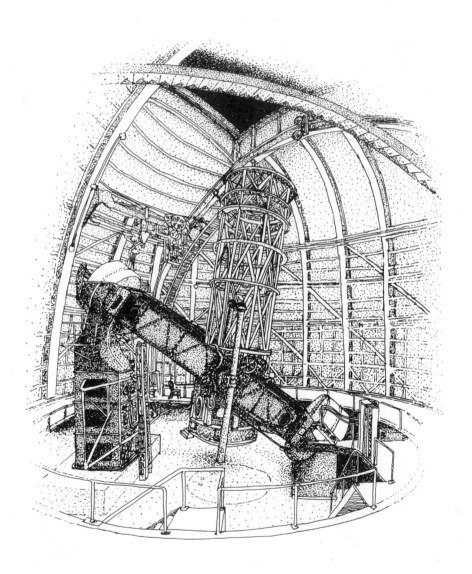

3 | HOW DREAMS WORK: THE INSIDE STORY

*This we know. The earth does not belong to man;
man belongs to the earth. Whatever befalls the
earth befalls the sons of earth. This we know. All
things are connected like the blood which unites
one family. All things are connected.*

Chief Seattle

It becomes clear as soon as we start to work with dreams that there are a vast
number of different types of dreams. When Elias Howe dreamed about how
to design his sewing machine needle, he was not having the same dream as a
the young teenage boy who dreams he is flying through the air on his bicycle. And
neither of these dreams is like a three-year-old's nightmare of being chased by a
huge, terrible monster. It makes sense, then, to ask about the types of dreams we
are likely to encounter and what purpose each type serves.

Before we discuss these two subjects, however, we need to repeat a very
important point which, until now, we have only briefly mentioned. All dreams are
guidance dreams. Every dream brings us a message from our higher consciousness—that wise, mature, enlightened part of ourselves which we call the Master
Teacher. The Master Teacher within us knows what is right and necessary for us,

but it often speaks in such a "still, small voice" that we don't hear it. In fact, some of us may not even be aware that it's there.

DREAM ALERT

If you are someone who doesn't normally remember your dreams but you have one you do remember, it stands to reason that you are supposed to pay attention to it.

On the other hand, if you tend to remember your dreams but you don't work with them, and you notice that you have the same dream several nights in a row, again, you would be well-advised to try to figure out what it's saying.

And lest you get overconfident: if you not only remember your dreams but also work with them faithfully, and you find yourself having the same dream more than once, you probably need to re-consider what you thought the dream was telling you. After all, your higher consciousness would not hit you over and over again with the same message if you clearly understood it. Your unconscious could be saying: "Listen up—this is important; now get it right!"

We spend a lot of time (and money) in this culture searching for our "inner-child" and trying to help that child—which is our self—express itself and free itself from demands of the past. We read many books on the subject, and we hear from professionals and many others who offer help in the journey. We're told that, once we acknowledge that child within, he or she can grow and mature. This should free us to become the mature, well-adjusted person we wish to be.

However, there are other ways to reach this same enlightenment. For example, with the same investment in time—but a much smaller investment in money—we can learn to meditate. Or, by working with our dreams, we can put ourselves directly in contact with our Master Teacher, the part of us that knows us best.

As we become more aware of the information and assistance available in our dreams, we are given more assistance from that source; the old axiom, "the rich get richer," is at work here. When we ask a question of our dreams, using a "pillow message," for example, we get an answer from our higher consciousness. We may not like that answer, we may not accept it, and/or we may not understand it, but it is there for us. Let us give you an example.

Guidance from Dreams: An Example

To find your own way is to follow your own bliss.
This involves analysis, watching yourself and seeing where
the real deep bliss is—not the quick little excitement,
but the real, deep, life-filling bliss.

Joseph Campbell, *The Power of Myth*

A number of years ago, a young friend of ours lost her wedding ring set. It contained a very valuable marquis-cut diamond, and she was most upset about it. She looked everywhere and became more and more upset when she didn't find it. Finally, she came to us for help. We told her to ask for help through a dream and explained how to do this using some of the steps we presented in Chapter 2 of this workbook. Then we sent her home. The next day she called to say that she had done what we said and had a dream that night, but she was sure the dream had nothing to do with her rings.

Tell us the dream, we said, and let us be the judge of that.

She dreamed that she was going to a Safeway [Safeway is a large chain of supermarkets in the southwest, though there was no Safeway in her town] and there was a marquee over the store entrance which read, "Vienna sausages, 2 cans for 69¢." Inside the store, she took a grocery cart and started going up and down the aisles, putting the food she selected under the basket instead of in the basket.

How, she wondered, could this dream have anything to do with her rings? "Ah," said Jim, "it's clear that the dream is about your rings: in your dream, there's a 'marquee' over the grocery store entrance—stores like this don't usually have marquees, so we need to make the marquee/marquis connection. And we aren't at an A&P or a Kroger's, we're at a Safeway, so there's a message that the rings are safe. Because the setting is a grocery store, I feel the rings will probably be found in an area or a place connected with food. Also, the dream seems to be saying that they're under a basket: have you got baskets in your kitchen or somewhere else in your house where you deal with food?"

"No," said our friend, "we don't have baskets in the house, and I've looked all over the kitchen, and there's no sign of the rings—I *knew* this wouldn't work, and I know I'll never find those rings, and I just—"

"It'll be OK. I want you to go home and look one more time. Look especially hard for baskets—and then look under the baskets. We will find those rings, I'm sure of it. They're 'safe,' after all."

Off she went, not at all convinced but willing to give it one more try. That very night she called us, as happy and excited as she had been miserable and unhappy that morning. "We found them! We found them!" she said. We asked her to tell us what happened.

"Well," she said, "I went home and looked again—and again—and still didn't find them. I finally went crying to my husband, who asked me to tell him all about it. When I told him my dream and what you both had said about it, he immediately went straight to the kitchen sink, opened the doors to the cabinet *under* the sink, took apart the pipe in there—you know, the one that curves to catch stuff—and there they were!"

"Of course," Jim said, "the dream was telling us that the rings were in the 'p-trap' under the sink. The little basket in the sink that keeps food from going down the drain: *that* was the basket that the dream was showing us!" Now, no doubt you have figured out all of the other clues which the dream presented. The most obvious is that we needed to be looking under things, because in the dream she was putting the food in an unusual spot, *under* the grocery cart basket rather than in it.

Also, as her husband pointed out to us in our "Monday-morning quarter-backing" session, a Vienna sausage can is an unusual size, much smaller than, say, a can of carrots, and in fact is just about the diameter of the pipes under a normal sink. Moreover, he reminded us, those pipes have an unusual configuration, sort of like the shape a "6" and a "9" make: and that was exactly the price shown for the Vienna sausagaes on the marquee.

It must be obvious by now that one of the steps we take in interpreting our dreams is to look for the details that are unusual or out-of-the-ordinary. But we'll talk more about that in Chapter 4; what we want to stress here is that our friend found her ring because she asked a part of her which *knew the answer*, her higher consciousness, to tell her where it was.

We are all aware that we access a pitifully small portion of the potential which exists in our brains. At some level which she couldn't consciously reach, our friend knew exactly where she left her rings. Some part of her knew exactly when she nudged the little saucer they were resting in just enough to cause them to slip into the sudsy water in the sink below; when she lifted the basket out to let the water go down the drain more quickly, the rings went along with the soapsuds. And she "knew" this.

But she could not *consciously* recall that moment. It happened at a level below or beyond consciousness, and the overwhelming emotion she was feeling helped to block her memory or recall. All she needed to do was to ask herself for help, go to sleep, and let her higher consciousness tackle the job.

This is just one example; there are hundreds and thousands of others that illustrate how helpful and important the messages can be that we receive through dreams. So, first of all, we must understand that all dreams bring us some kind of guidance from our higher consciousness. Then we need to look at the different types of dreams through which that guidance might come to us. And finally, we need to be sure we understand what kind of help we can expect from these various kinds of dreams. When we know all of this, we will be ready, in Chapter 4, to practice this new skill, to actually tackle some dreams and see if we can understand how they "work."

Alan asked for a dream to answer a question which was deeply troubling him: "Why am I not happy?" He received the following dream:

I dreamed I was walking along picking up coins: pennies here, nickels there, dimes and quarters all over the place. Finally, I had whole handfuls of small change.

He had received his answer: he needed to find ways to "change" his life—small ways and large ways, since we saw him picking up small coins and large ones. He needed to make lots and lots—handfuls—of these changes.

Most people who deal with dreams as we do have established their own way of categorizing dream types. We're no different: for us a dream fits into one of seven categories. In alphabetical order, the categories are anxiety, physical, psychic (or pre-cognitive), self-awareness (or personal development), spiritual, warning, and wish-fulfillment. Each of these types is important in its own way, and each provides the dreamer with a particular kind of assistance. Let us look at these at some length, along with several examples of each and an explanation of what kind of help each type can give.

Anxiety Dreams

Dreams are the touchstones of our character.

Henry David Thoreau

Most of us worry, though we don't all worry to the same degree. We worry about whether we look our best, whether the plane will crash, whether our child is progressing in school, whether we left the iron on, whether some symptom or other is serious, whether our efforts at work are being appreciated, and so on. It is no surprise that much of this worry carries over to our dreams at night. Thus we see our dreams often reflecting or revealing what has occupied our waking minds. Let's look at a few examples, starting with one from Carol.

> *My husband and I are walking uphill through a park. On top of the hill, there is a rose garden with a circular walk around it. The roses are dead now; it's winter time. We walk around the garden, talking about how beautiful the roses will be in the summer and how we want to come back then and look at them. When we get to the end of the circle, the path goes back down again. I suddenly panic because the way looks so steep. I turn to my husband and say, "Oh, I can't go down this hill: I'm going to fall and break my neck!" But he holds on to me and says, "Don't worry, I'm going to be right here, and I'm not going to let you fall." When I wake up, I'm full of emotion.*

This is a very significant dream for Carol. It has to do with a cycle which is occurring in her life, as we can see by the circular path around the rose garden. Her life, like that of the garden, is now at a point of dormancy; both are preparing for the birth of a new cycle. Her children are teenagers, and she may now be considering taking a new step, perhaps getting a job outside of her home. Carol understands that, as the cycle moves along, the roses will begin to bloom. In other words, the changes that are coming will be beneficial and beautiful for her.

However, she is also suddenly aware that there are some difficult periods ahead before that time arrives. She faces that steep downhill path, where things might get going faster than she is comfortable with. But the dream is telling her that there is a great deal of reassurance and support available for her from her husband—and from knowing that the roses *will* be beautiful when they bloom.

At first, as we helped Carol work through this dream, she expressed surprise and some denial. She hadn't been aware that she was at all anxious about this upcoming stage in her life. But as we questioned her—both about her dream and about where she was in her life—and suggested some connections based on her responses, she became more and more positive that we were pointed in the right direction. Yet, she sounded relieved at the very positive feelings that were evident at the end of the dream.

This is a classic anxiety dream and clearly illustrates the two ways in which such dreams can offer us guidance. First, they frequently make us face and finally accept the fact that we are fearful about something. Often, when we face change, we become fearful about it. Because we think such fears are silly or inappropriate, or because we feel that we must not appear fearful to those around us, we may force such feelings out of our conscious mind. The dream brings them to the surface in a non-threatening environment. After all, no one knows what we dream—unless or until we decide to tell them. The dream gently, and sometimes not so gently, puts the fear in front of us and says, "Here. You haven't wanted to admit this consciously, but it's really time to face it."

The other way anxiety dreams can be helpful is that they often provide a "fix" for the situation which is causing the anxiety. This might be an actual solution or simply reassurance that the dreamer will have the support needed to get through the situation. Trevor gave us an interesting dream that will serve to illustrate this second purpose. His aunt, to whom he feels very close, is in a nursing home. Her children don't visit her very much anymore, and he feels very angry about this. Trevor told us:

> *I dreamed that I was walking down the corridor of the nursing home to visit my aunt, dressed as a big chicken, wearing a green crocheted sweater.*

As we talked with Trevor about the dream, we both seemed to agree that it was telling him that he was being a "chicken" by not going to his cousins to tell them how he felt about their abandonment of their mother. That inerpretation seemed pretty satisfactory to all three of us, so we left it at that.

But Pat found that the dream stayed with in her, and that she continued to work at it for a day or two after it had supposedly been interpreted. Taking this as a clue that the dream's true meaning had not yet been reached, she began to search for other reasons Trevor would dream about himself as a big chicken. When she saw him again, she asked how he felt about his aunt and the nursing home. "I hate it," he said quickly. "My stomach flops over every time I walk in there. Sometimes I feel so bad I have to turn around and walk out for a while."

Pat asked one more question: "What are you afraid of?" Trevor looked at her for a minute and then answered with a surprised tone in his voice, "I guess I didn't realize it, but I'm really afraid that I'll wind up like my aunt, alone, unvisited, in a nursing home somewhere. That really terrifies me, that I'll end like that."

There it was, the "Aha!" that had really been missing after our first go-round with this dream. Trevor knew he was being a bit of a chicken in not talking things out with his cousins. But that wasn't causing him the most anxiety. Prior to the dream, he didn't realize how worried he was about his future. He had just turned fifty, was unmarried, and was feeling more and more vulnerable to the consequences of age. The dream helped him recognize his concern about this aspect of his life so that he was able to start dealing with it on a conscious level.

There was more help in the dream, too: the sweater, which was green to symbolize healing, provided protection and shelter. But most of all, in the humor of the chicken costume, there was a message to Trevor to lighten up, look around for the fun and joy in his life. Deep-seated, heavy-hearted anxiety was not the answer.

Thus, in Trevor's dream, the comfort that the green sweater provides and the light-heartedness of the dream help to show him both that he'll be OK and that he's being silly to worry. And in Carol's dream, she understands that her husband will be there for her through the changes that are coming. Of course, she probably knew that all along. But to have him state it so clearly and openly in the dream provides extra reassurance for her. She, like the roses, will bloom beautifully.

Here's another anxiety dream, this one from a new mother. This dream works similarly to Carol's dream in some ways, slightly differently in other ways:

> *This is a recurring dream, which I first had when my son was about five months old. He's now two, and I still have the dream, though not as often as I did at first. In my dream, my son is always getting ready to fall from a very great height—he's climbing through bars or something like that. Sometimes my husband is there with him, but he's not paying attention to the baby, and, for some reason, I'm not able to yell to my son. At other times, the baby is alone. I run to try to grab him, but I never make it. The baby always falls over the edge.*

Lately, I have this same kind of dream, but it's not one of falling, rather it's one of drowning. The baby falls into water, where I can't see him, and I go into the water, but I can't save him.

This mother is clearly anxious. We asked her how old she was and learned that she was over thirty and this was her first child. A certain amount of anxiety is normal for any mother, but hers was exaggerated.

In this dream, we see the baby falling at first, and later drowning. Checking in the dream dictionary in Chapter 5, we find that, in a broad, general sense, falling in dreams generally represents failing, while drowning symbolizes being in a situation—usually a very emotional situation—over one's head. Thus, the mother was not only worried about protecting her son from the actual physical dangers of falling or drowning; she was afraid her child would find himself in situations where he would fail or would be unable to manage things and she wouldn't be able to protect him in these situations.

The dreams also showed that the dreamer didn't feel her husband was aware or concerned enough about all of the dangers that the baby would be facing. As the dreams continued, as her child developed and became more important in her life, and as she became more aware of the many situations which he would face, her dreams became filled with emotion, symbolized by the water.

This mother was aware that she was worried about her child. However, she was not ready to see that her anxiety was excessive. As we discussed the various aspects of the dream, and particularly as we reminded her that this was a recurring dream, she began to change her mind. She began to see that, though she felt sure she could provide adequate protection for him at the age of two, she was quite concerned about her son in the future, when he would not be so closely under her supervision.

Consciously, she knew that growth automatically brought with it the chance of failure; but she began to see that unconsciously she was hoping to protect her child from even the smallest failures. She also admitted that she didn't feel her husband was worried about this as much as she felt he should be. She thought that, as their son grew older, she would be alone in trying to shield him from any possibility of harm.

Once the mother was made aware of the extent of her anxiety, she was able to begin to work through it. Her higher consciousness was saying to her: "Be aware that this is how you are feeling. Find the things you can do to diminish or eliminate this anxiety. Perhaps you could discuss the situation with your husband so that the two of you can make decisions now about how to handle things as your child grows older." As the dreamer begins to face her extreme anxiety in this way, it may be reduced to more normal levels, and she and her husband will be able to anticipate and avoid a potential conflict that they might otherwise face.

Anxiety dreams can also be prompted by small annoyances. For example, a dreamer may be confronted by swarms of bees or flies or ants, which show her in a very literal way that she is letting little things "bug" her. On the other hand, anxiety can also be expressed in nightmares. The falling baby dream qualifies as a nightmare, but so do dreams in which we are chased by ugly, monstrous beings. In these situations, we need to do two things: we need to understand that we have a strong fear or anxiety about something, and then we need to discover what that something is so that we can face it and reduce or eliminate the fear. As we have seen, our Master Teacher helps us in the first task: the messages are there in our dreams—all we have to do is recognize them. In Chapter 4, we'll learn how our Master Teacher can help us confront our fears and anxieties in dreams and thus overcome them.

Physical Dreams

Know thyself and nothing else too much.

Plato

In the late twentieth century, we're becoming aware ("re-aware" is a better word, since this is an awareness that we had several centuries ago) that there is much about our physical bodies that we can take responsibility for. Biofeedback and the use of positive thinking to help heal illnesses have shown us how much we can do to maintain our own health. And, not surprisingly, our dreams are one of the best sources of information about our physical deficiencies. If we are able to understand their messages, we can "doctor" ourselves—or be shown the right person to doctor us—and prevent, alleviate, or even cure some of our problems. Here are some dreams that illustrate how this works.

> *This a dream that has recurred a number of times throughout my life. I dream that a civil war is being fought in a large Southern mansion. Soldiers are running around the mansion, up and down stairs and through all the corridors, fighting each other. The soldiers' jackets are red and white, and there are a lot of injuries and much blood.*

Our first question to this dreamer was, "Are you dealing with any problems involving your blood or circulation?" She responded that she was often diagnosed as anemic, and we knew immediately that she was being warned about that anemic condition in these recurring dreams. Of course, we couldn't be sure that there was a correlation between the dreams and the occurrence of the spells of anemia, since this dreamer did not keep a journal. But we felt that such a correlation did exist.

We found a number of clues in the dream that told us it was pointing to a physical problem. First of all, the setting is a mansion, a house. It is widely understood that a house in a dream symbolizes the body, the "house" that shelters each of us. Then there is the idea of a "civil" war, a war that takes place entirely within a state or country's boundaries rather than between two separate entities. But the most significant clue is the red- and white-jacketed soldiers. Here we literally see the red and white corpuscles of the blood running through body, fighting with each other. With anemia, the white blood cells attack the red ones, resulting in the weakened condition of our blood. The dreamer's unconscious understood this process and tried to bring it to her attention so she could begin treatment before the disease got out of hand.

> *I dreamed last night that I was taking cheese to the cleaners.*

The clue that this is a physical dream is that it has to do with cleaning. Our dreams often point out something we need to do or to stop doing in order to restore our body's functions to their most efficient state; often such advice comes before we become consciously aware that there is something wrong. For example, many adults lack the enzyme necessary to digest milk. And most of us don't digest cheese well if it has been aged less than six months. So, for this dreamer, the advice was very simple: "Look at what you ate the day before—perhaps some inadequately aged cheese or some other milk product—and cleanse it out of your system."

This next dream clearly illustrates our body's ability to help us doctor ourselves. Our friend Bill had been hospitalized for a stroke. While in the hospital, he had this dream. It upset him so much that his wife called us and asked what the dream might mean.

> I dreamed I was in my car, and I drove off a high bridge into water. I was in the car as it sank into the water, and I could see the water level rising outside the car windows.

This was a classic physical dream. Bill's car represents his body, and it was clear that he was drowning. Our sense was that his lungs were filling up and he was coming down with pneumonia. With this information, his wife encouraged his doctors to check his condition, and, sure enough, that was exactly what was happening. He was aware on an unconscious level of what was going on in his body; the dream allowed the knowledge to reach his conscious mind in time to correct the condition.

Pat had an important experience with a physical dream. For more than a year, she had the same dream nearly once a month; each time, she awoke feeling very concerned. Her sense was that there was a problem with one of her breasts. During this time, Pat went to three different doctors, none of whom detected any lump or found any other problem. Since she was in her early thirties at the time, none of the doctors suggested that she have a mammogram.

However, even after these examinations, the dream continued to recur; Pat found herself waking from it with more and more emotion. Finally, she went to the local Women's Center, where she insisted that she receive a mammogram. When the results of the mammogram were examined, a small growth was found in her right breast, and the lab tests showed that it was cancerous. Her doctor quickly made arrangements to remove the lump; it was so small that surgeons had to use x-rays beforehand to find and pinpoint the lump so that they would be able to locate it during the operation.

There was a happy ending: the lump was removed in time, and the breast was saved. Perhaps the happiest part of the ending was Pat's opportunity to say to her doctor, "I told you that lump was there," and her doctor's genuine amazement at her method of discovery. While we should state strongly that we don't recommend that dreams *replace* regular self-examination, we do say that dreams can certainly provide a most helpful supplemental service.

Psychic/Precognitive Dreams

*The fundamental change will occur with
the change of mind in the dreamer.*

A Course in Miracles

Precognitive dreams, dreams that tell us about events before we can possibly have knowledge of them, are probably the most well-known type of dream because they are so disturbing. A young boy dreams about an accident in which a man is killed and his companion uninjured, and the next day he sees a picture in the newspaper of the same accident which had happened almost a thousand miles away as he was dreaming about it. Abraham Lincoln dreams one night his corpse is laid out in the East Room of the White House—and a few days later he is assassinated. Many of the dreams from the Bible contain predictions of events which will befall the dreamer or those close to him or her. One well-documented instance of such precognitive dreaming is shown below.

On Friday October 21, 1966, the people of Britain were stunned by news of an appalling tragedy. At 9:15 that morning in the little Welsh mining village of Aberfan, a mountain of coal waste avalanched and buried the town's school. The waste weighed a half million tons, and had been loosened by two days of heavy rain. More than 140 people, most of them children who had just assembled for classes, died under the black landslide.

One of the children who died, nine-year-old Eryl Mai Jones, had told her mother the day before that she dreamed she had gone to school "and there was no school there. Something black had come down all over it." During that night of the nineteenth when Eryl Mai had her dream, and also during the night of the twentieth, several other people in various parts of England had disturbing dreams that seemed to contain premonitions of the disaster. One woman dreamed of a mountain flowing downward and a child running and screaming. Another saw a screaming child in a telephone booth and another child being followed by a "black billowing mass." A third woman saw children at school dressed in Welsh national costume ascending to heaven. An elderly man dreamed of the word Aberfan spelled out in bright light, though at the time he didn't know of the existence of the Welsh village and the word meant nothing to him.

After the tragedy, the press launched a survey to gather information on premonitions of the disaster. It revealed that many other people had had apparent dream premonitions of the event for a period of some two weeks before it happened. One woman had a dream of "screaming children buried by an avalanche of coal in a mining village." Another dreamed of "hundreds of black horses thundering down a hillside dragging hearses." A young man in Kent woke on October 17 with a vague sense of approaching catastrophe that remained with him the rest of the week. He told a woman in his office that "On Friday something terrible connected with death is going to happen." A Mr. Alexander Venn told his wife the same thing. He found that for days his thoughts kept turning to the subject of coal dust, and he drew a sketch of a head surrounded by a black cloud…

In all, thirty-six dream premonitions of the event were received in response to the survey.

From Dream Worlds
"Dreaming the Future," pp. 112-114.

Dreams such as these occur each night all over the world. The important question to ask, though, is how can we know whether we are dreaming a precognitive dream or merely a dream that uses startling or frightening images, such as a fire or a plane crash, to give us some information about the events which we have been dealing with in our lives. To find the answer to this question, which is not a simple one, let's look at a dream:

> *I was in the office of Chris Barrett [a well-known doctor in the town where the dreamer lived] and he was lying on the floor. He had been knocked out—or killed—and robbed; his drug cabinet had been broken into and there were drugs scattered all over the floor.*

Here was a real person, a real setting, and an event which could really happen. Was this a precognitive dream? If so, the dreamer would want to warn the doctor and the police right away that a break-in was possible. Because there was nothing out of the ordinary about the setting, the character, or the event in the dream, it could potentially be a precognitive dream. However, the dreamer's name was Christine, Chris for short, and we knew that she was in touch with a spiritual guide who represented some of her male aspects and who was named Christopher—which can also be shortened to Chris. We were also aware that lately Christine had been taking a great deal of medication for several different symptoms.

We posed several questions to Christine and then observed as she considered them for a minute. "Aha!" We could see the light of realization dawning in her face. She was the one who stated what we all realized: "All of this medication I've been taking lately has knocked out or incapacitated—or even killed—any communication between me and my assertive self, my male side! He can't reach me because he's been so sedated lately." Here was an interpretation of the dream which really spoke to Christine, bringing her to an "Aha!" of recognition. So we felt fairly certain that there would be no article in tomorrow's paper, or any time soon, that Dr. Barrett's office had been ransacked.

But—and we must add this caution—we can never be absolutely positive that dreams about real people in real settings are not precognitive. Only time will truly tell. So, the only way to answer the question, "Is this dream precognitive or not?" is to first make whatever connections can be made between the dreamer and the dream situation. Draw the parallels between what happens in the dream and what's happening in the dreamer's life. Then wait for that "Aha!" feeling. If it doesn't come, you may need to consider the possibility that you are indeed having a prophetic dream.

Precognitive dreams contain some notable characteristics which will be helpful in determining whether or not your dream falls into this category. Often precognitive dreams are unusual in that they do not focus on a particular person. Rather, when people appear in such a precognitive dream, they appear in groups, crowds, or masses. The viewpoint of the dreamer is usually that of an observer removed from the actions of the dream itself, as if the dreamer were recording scenes for a movie from a crane suspended far above the action of the dream. Indeed, the intent of such dreams seems to be similar to that of documentary films: purely to provide information.

Perhaps the most significant difference between these precognitive dreams and other, "normal" anxiety dreams has to do with the feeling the dreamer has upon waking. A dreamer who has had an anxiety dream in which she or a loved one is in imminent danger of drowning, for example, wakes with an overwhelming feeling of terror. One moment, she is drowning, splashing frantically to keep from sinking, or trying desperately to rescue someone else from this horrible fate; the next moment, she is awake, tense, perhaps breathing shallowly and quickly, with a quickened heartbeat, and often she is disoriented.

However, upon waking from the particular kind of precognitive dream we are discussing here, the dreamer is affected in a very different way. Remember: the content of the dream has been presented straightforwardly, the way a movie is projected upon a screen. Frantic and desperate scenes may have been part of the "movie" which the dreamer has watched, but the dreamer has not been involved in them. Thus, rather than waking with intense fear or anxiety, as well as with all the physical symptoms that accompany these strong emotions, the dreamer instead wakens feeling a strong and immediate call to action. Note that the precognitive dreamer's feelings are no less intense than those of an anxiety dreamer; but, whereas the anxiety dreamer's focus is on what just happened in the dream, the precognitive dreamer's focus is on what needs to be done and who needs to be told.

It is especially important to write down precognitive dreams. Once it's in your journal, it will never be lost, and you can go back later to corroborate your premonition, should it correspond with real life.

Self-Awareness/Personal Development Dreams

Everything that irritates us about others can
lead us to an understanding of ourselves.

Carl Jung

Self-awareness dreams can be described as advice from our higher consciousness, our Master Teacher, on how to be a better person tomorrow: sort of a dreamer's guide to good behavior. Whether we need a little nudge back onto a higher path or a big dose of self-improvement, our superconscious will be the first to let us know if we are ready to listen. Let's look at two dreams, one with a small lesson, the other with a more significant message.

> *The first dream came during an afternoon nap. Avis, the dreamer, was tired and annoyed as she drifted to sleep, though there appeared to be no specific cause for this annoyance. In her dream, Avis and another woman are sitting at a table. Avis's daughter, younger in the dream than she actually is, enters the kitchen, chewing an exceptionally large wad of gum. She takes the gum out and sticks it under the kitchen table. Her mother criticizes her for this, asking why she did it. Her daughter retorts, "So I can come back and chew it later." Avis says, "Don't do that. That is a nasty habit."*

This simple dream was, at first, difficult for the dreamer to understand. The other woman at the table was a hazy figure whom she could not identify, making it clear that the focus of the dream was on the actions of the daughter, an immature part of the dreamer herself. So Avis asked herself what she had been "chewing" on recently and what she might have "tabled" for another time. The answer came almost at once: she had had an argument the day before with her sister, who had made a remark Avis felt was unkind. She had "chewed" on this remark and, though hurt, had not responded immediately (she "tabled" her response), planning to find a cutting remark of her own as retaliation.

Here was a lesson from the higher, more mature part of herself, saying very clearly, "Don't do this. It is not a good thing for you to do." She had not gone to sleep consciously thinking about it, but it had surely been underlying her annoyance. Often, we "know better" but we forget what we know, and we need this kind of reminder from our higher self. Paula is the dreamer of our second dream:

> I am in a sorority house. I move from table to table in the house, noticing that the other sorority members are performing service work at the tables. I go to my room, where I see myself pick up a putty knife. Someone comes by the room, says, "Don't," takes the knife away and continues down the hall. Then I have a paring knife in my hand, and the same thing happens: someone comes by, says, "Don't," takes the knife away, and goes on down the hall. Next, I have a butcher knife, and finally a large hara-kiri knife. Each time I am told not to do whatever I plan to do by someone who then leaves. Finally, though, I see myself enter the room. My hair and my clothes are lighter than I usually wear, and I am carrying a huge samurai sword. I begin to duel with this "lighter" self, but my "lighter" self sees the absurdity of the situation, because the samurai sword is so much bigger than my hara-kiri knife. So my "lighter" self wins.

This dream has to do with Paula's tendency to "cut" herself down with negative remarks, such as telling herself that she doesn't give enough of herself. We see this as she leaves the others who are performing service and goes to her room where she must deal with a succession of larger and more dangerous knives. Her friends, the "someones" who pass her door, have been trying to stop her, but her negativity has only been accelerating to a level that could now be very destructive. At this point, her higher or "lighter" self enters the dream with a much stronger weapon. It is as if she were being told, "Hey, if cutting yourself down was something that needed doing, I can do it much more effectively than you can. Lighten up, Paula, and get back to work. You're fine."

Here is another dream which provided a mother with some important and helpful information about her son:

> *My son and I are walking along a very busy street in our neighborhood which is unusually packed with pedestrians. I say to my son, "Why are we walking? Let's go and get the car." And he says, "No, let's go on." Then, suddenly, I can't find him. So I get on a bus (normally you can't catch a bus on this street) and begin to look for my son. When the bus stops, I look around and say to the bus driver, "Where am I?" and he says, "You're in Orange," and I say, "Well, I can't be." He says, "Come with me, ma'am," and he takes me into this palace, this beautiful, calming palace. But I tell him I need to get back home. Then the phone rings, and he answers it and says to me, "Are you Mrs. So-and-so?" and I say yes. The person on the phone is my son.*

This dream begins on a road, a setting which indicates that the dream will focus on the dreamer's path through life. The street is unusually crowded, which is perhaps a representation of the dreamer's own busy life. The dreamer wants to take an easier form of transportation, her car, but the son wants to walk; he wants to do things the hard way.

But suddenly she can't find him. There is a sense here that the communication between the two has been interrupted—by the son, probably, since he is the one who disappears. She gets on a bus—a vehicle which she cannot control herself—and she is taken to a strange place. She asks a simple question: "Where am I?" As we will see in Chapter 4, questions asked in dreams must be very carefully noted, as well as the answers received, because they provide vital information for the dreamer. Here, her question expresses confusion—and the answer, "You're in Orange," does not clear things up. In fact, she flatly denies that she is there.

This dreamer had some trouble with the significance of Orange when we were working with her. She knew of a city named Orange in the state where she lived but it had no connection for her. Orange was one of the colors for the state university, and her son had been thinking about college, but he was not particularly interested in attending that university. Finally, Pat suggested that they look at the color orange and what it represents in general. Orange is a primal color, a gonadal color, and it usually deals with sexual feelings. The mother was plunked down in Orange/orange and then led by the bus driver into a lovely, romantic palace.

This struck a chord with the mother, and she told us that the boy had recently asked a girl to the homecoming dance. It was the first time he had ever asked a girl out, and the mother was understandably anxious about the situation. He would be dealing with adolescent energies in a very romantic setting, and he would need some clear, explicit communication from his mother in order to handle the situation properly.

The final corroboration for this is the ringing telephone. When a telephone rings in a dream, it is not merely the dreamer's unconscious signaling a need for the dreamer to communicate; it is a very specific call for communication directly from the person on the other end—in this case, the son. Though the son may not be signaling it consciously, on another level he is making a very clear request for guidance from his mother.

Such dreams offer us the kind of assistance we are always hoping our best friends will give us—yet when we hear it from friends, we are often defensive and quick to deny that we exhibit certain behavior. Similarly, when we receive such advice in dreams we are often just as quick to deny that the dream really refers to us.

To help our receptivity to these messages, we need to remember two things: first, this is strictly between us and our higher self. No one else ever needs to know that we've had our knuckles rapped, so to speak, for our behavior. The other thing to remember is that, if we ask for guidance but close our minds to it when it is given to us, either the guidance will come again and again until we do pay attention to it, or it will stop coming altogether because the unconscious senses that we are not serious in our quest. It is very important that we remain open to those "postcards from the subconscious," if we want to continue to receive them.

Here's another dream which gives the dreamer a different way of looking at a situation. A change is definitely needed here, but the dreamer has failed to see the need. One night, she dreamed this dream:

I have a golden screw in the center of my back, and I can't reach it. I ask my husband to use the screwdriver on the dresser to help me remove it, because it's causing me great pain. He refuses to help me.

The golden screw is a symbol full of meaning: it's gold, which relates to wealth, finances, money; it's a screw, which is a pun on being cheated, as well as a crude pun on the sex act; and it's stuck in the dreamer's back, where she didn't see it coming and can't protect herself from it or even get it out. Her husband won't help her remove it. This is a woman who is being held in a situation that is bad for her, that is causing her pain and perhaps cheating her out of any real happiness and a chance at a good life. She is also prostituting herself for money and financial security.

She had been unable to face the danger of her situation before, but this dream was so clear and compelling that she could not avoid it. Clearly, her husband would not help her; she would need to ask someone else for help. But that golden screw must be removed at all costs.

Spiritual Dreams

Nothing outside yourself can save you;
Nothing outside yourself can give you peace.

Workbook, *A Course in Miracles*

Spiritual dreams give us wonderful opportunities to experience feelings that we can't usually experience in our everyday lives. For example, many people have dreams in which they fly (often, though not always, without a plane or any other mechanical help). Most people tell of the wonderful sensations they experience in these dreams, the exhilaration, the sense of freedom, the feeling that they are truly more than the mundane earth-bound creature that is their identity during waking hours.

Another classic spiritual dream is one in which the dreamer sees himself or herself standing with Christ or the Buddha or some other holy personage. As with the flying dreams, the most notable element of these dreams is the wonderful feeling of spiritual exhilaration with which the dreamer awakens. It feels like the equivalent of an actual blessing from a spiritual being. Often such dreams come to us as a clear and unambiguous reward, perhaps after a long, especially stressful period or after achieving some especially meaningful goal.

A spiritual dream can also take the form of more "normal," story-telling type. For example, here's a dream we worked with several years ago:

> *In this dream, I'm at a university in Europe in a long line of students ascending a steep hill. At the top of the hill is a shoe repair shop, and all the students are there to pick up their shoes, which have had the soles replaced. About halfway up, I come across an obstacle I can't get past: it's like a twisted vine, a bramble with thorns, and snakes are running through it, and on each side are alligators. I can't get over it to keep going, and a man in front of me turns around and sees that I'm in trouble. He's very kind, but I don't remember his face—I don't know if I didn't look at it or if I just can't remember it. Anyway, he picks me up and helps me over this obstacle.*

Though the dream is not the classic flying dream or "standing-with-Christ" type of dream, this is clearly a spiritual dream. We see this dreamer in a foreign country, in an unfamiliar place. She is at an institute of higher [more spiritual] learning, where she is studying something which she must exert a real effort to learn—this is shown by the long climb up a steep hill. The goal is a shoe shop where soles [souls] are replaced [renewed], but there is a seemingly insurmountable obstacle in the way. There is no way around it—until a kind stranger steps in and provides the necessary assistance.

In fact, when we offered this explanation to the dreamer, she corroborated all of it. Lately, she said, she had been doing a lot of studying about reincarnation and about the possibility of the earth being a school for the soul, one that we leave and return to in different lives. Because she was raised within a very traditional religion that discouraged this kind of thinking, she had been experiencing a philosophical struggle, and there were many obstacles which she needed to overcome. In this context, the dream was clearly providing encouragement by telling her, "You will receive help; persevere in your efforts, and you will succeed."

Here is another very common type of spiritual dream. It was given to us by a woman whose aunt had died five months earlier after a long illness. The aunt was very dear to the woman. The evening before she died, the woman became quite emotional in thinking about her aunt and decided that she should go by and visit her the next day. But early that morning, before she could make her visit, the aunt passed away.

> That night I dreamed that I saw her face. She was smiling, and there was no pain any more. I told her she looked good, she looked happy, and she said, "Yes, I'm well now, and it's OK. You don't need to worry any more." And then she said, referring to my son by a nickname that only she used, "Take care of Whosit for me."

This dream needs no interpreting. In fact, it's almost an experience, rather than a dream. It is a loving gift which the dreamer received from her beloved aunt as she was leaving this plane. A contact was made; the aunt was saying, "I'm happy, I'm well, I'm healed," and at the same time she was also saying to the niece, "Now continue your life, do your job well, and take care of little Whosit for me."

This is a beautiful gift, which has a double purpose: though the dreamer had been unable to make her final visit with the aunt, they were together and "visited," in a sense, in the dream. In a larger way, this very vivid message from the aunt will be of immeasurable help as the dreamer deals with her loss.

Spiritual dreams, in all of their forms, are the blessings we are given as we drift into the unconscious state. They are like a reward at the end of the day or at the end of a period when we've been working diligently on something. We're given a sense of freedom, of flight, a real spiritual lift. Such dreams are more spiritual than others because we see ourselves totally in tune with nature and with others in a deep and timeless way.

Warning Dreams

The great aim of education is not knowledge but action.

Herbert Spencer

Warning dreams are among the best-known of the dream types. Most of us look at our dreams first to see if they hold some important information about the day ahead of us. Should we change our flight plans? Will we have some kind of accident? Is something unpleasant awaiting us at work? In fact, our dreams often do counsel us about what we can expect. For example, the following dream seems "cute" on the surface, but it has a clear caution for Kitty, the dreamer.

> *This was an unusual dream compared to the dreams I usually have. It was very bright, vivid, and colorful. Somehow, in the dream, I became aware that a lizard had come to live in my home. It wasn't a mean or scary lizard, but it was a dragon-like lizard. When I first got it, it was very small, and it came in a little basket. It would turn over and let me rub its belly. It was bright green, but when it turned over, its belly was a beautiful yellow. It would talk to me and I would talk to it. But it kept getting bigger and bigger and bigger, and nobody around me seemed concerned that I had this huge lizard.*

We asked Kitty to give us an adjective to describe how she would normally think about a lizard. She said that, though this lizard was a very friendly, happy lizard, she would be very frightened in "real life." Furthermore, when we asked if she was married, she said no, but that she had a new boyfriend who was a friend-ly and happy sort of guy. "Oh, yes," she added, "and he does like to have his belly rubbed."

It was obvious that the dream was about something that was coming into her home, and the new boyfriend was a most likely candidate. In the dream, the situa-tion starts out very small, not at all threatening [the little bright green lizard], but Kitty's unconscious perceives that this seemingly harmless situation has the poten-tial to become a problem [a dragon]. There's a bit of anxiety involved here but more humor than anything else.

The lizard's changing colors suggest the characteristics of a chameleon—that changeability which allows a creature to blend inconspicuously into its surround-ings. Such creatures seem never to show their "true colors." Kitty's unconscious was warning her that, while this individual at first seemed cuddly, happy, and friendly, after he'd been brought into the home, he had the capacity to become something quite different than expected.

Thus, Kitty was given information through her dream which could help her make decisions about her relationship. She was shown that something which at the start seemed cute and humorous *might* turn into something she really couldn't handle. This message gave her an opportunity to think things through. It's important to notice, though, that everything in the dream was kept light-hearted. The dragon never actually hurt or even frightened Kitty—and no one else seemed to notice its presence. Clearly, no one was going to criticize or condemn her for whatever choice she made regarding her relationship. She alone needed to make a decision.

Here's another warning dream that isn't so humorous, one which a woman named Belle gave us over the telephone during a radio talk show:

> *I dreamed that I was sitting in the waiting room of a lawyer's office, and I was talking to the woman who was going to go before me to see the lawyer. She was probably close to my age, in her mid-thirties, and she had a business having to do with autographs. She would get*

autographs from celebrities on paper and then put them on T-shirts. The lawyer turned out to be my grandmother, who died very suddenly in a car wreck thirty years ago, when I was six. When she was alive, she had very black hair, but in the dream her hair was shorter, salt-and-pepper colored, and very curly, as if it had been permed. I never did get in to see her, and that was the end of the dream.

We felt this was a warning dream because of the presence of the grand-mother, someone whom Belle had no contact with in the present. Often dreams include recently deceased relatives or friends (or even famous people who have died and whom we never personally knew), because they are on our minds. As time passes, our memories of them become more one-dimensional: we remember Uncle Harold because he always used to wink at us, and Aunt Kate because she always hugged us too tightly. In this way, the presence of Belle's grandmother in her dream would be a short-hand way of conveying some advice, a warning; she would represent a higher, wiser part of Belle than would be represented by, say, her mother or her sister.

The grandmother's wisdom is further emphasized by her position in the dream as a lawyer (which she never was) and the fact that she has gray hair in the dream (though she never did). The woman that Belle talks to in the waiting room is not someone Belle identifies or names, and so she likely represents Belle herself—she is even the same age as Belle. In sum, we see that Belle is consulting a lawyer, a professional, about her business, which has to do with signatures.

It's a short step from there to understanding that the dream was warning Belle that she should be cautious if she were to become involved with any business which might require a signature. She should be very leery about signing a contract or a similar legal paper. If such a situation were to arise, the dream seemed to be warning Belle not to move forward without getting some professional advice about the move.

Again, we seemed to have found the "Aha!" interpretation: Belle told us that she was currently involved in some legal work with a company which she and her husband partly owned, and that the situation was a very bad one. The dream message to her seemed clear and timely: Don't sign anything without competent legal guidance.

Wish-Fulfillment Dreams

I Have Abandoned My Search for Truth and
Am Now Looking for a Good Fantasy
—Book title, Ashley Brilliant

Much of Freud's original work on dreams and dream interpretation has come under fire or been set aside. For example, he felt that dreams served the purpose of wish fulfillment and that most of the wishes had a sexual foundation. As we have noted, because of the times in which he lived, he did work with many dreams that were sexually oriented, and dreams today often have similar foundations. However, it is no longer felt that nearly all—or even most—dreams are rooted in sex.

But it is still accepted that dreams can often serve the purpose of wish fulfillment. Let's look at one which classically illustrates this. It was called in by a radio listener—let's call her Carla:

> I dreamed I received in the mail a beautifully engraved invitation to take tea at Buckingham Palace with Lady Diana. I was very excited, and I prepared myself, my hair, and my clothes very carefully for the event. I was picked up by a limousine and arrived at the palace with much fanfare. There were servants everywhere; I was escorted to a gorgeous room where the tea was served. My every wish and desire was immediately catered to. Lady Di was beautiful; at one point, her children came into the room, well-mannered and beautifully dressed. They stayed a few moments and then were taken out by their Nanny. I hated for the dream to end.

We knew almost right away what the dream was all about. As we questioned Carla, we found that she was a single parent of two small children. She worked all day and went to school at night. She almost never had a moment for herself and was constantly waiting on others. Her unconscious knew she needed a break, a little beauty, and some be-good-to-yourself time. The dream presented an engraved invitation to do just that. She awoke feeling refreshed and pleased—and ready to return to her routine with a revived outlook.

4 | WORKING THROUGH YOUR DREAMS: STEPS TO THE GREAT "AHA!"

There are many answers you have received but not yet heard.

A Course in Miracles

We are here, at last, ready to roll up our sleeves and get to work on a dream. First, we're going to work through a dream, one with a number of interesting symbols and quite a bit of information for the dreamer. We will look at the information we needed to make sense of the dream and the process we followed. Also we'll show you the basic two-page set up we use in the dream journal, which has been designed to help gather information and put it down on paper in the most useful format. Then we will look at several more dreams, which will be presented in the dream journal. We'll work through these, as well, to reach the dream message. From there, we invite you to practice your new-found skills with your own dreams.

Let's get to work. We'll work with one of Pat's dreams, which tend to have several scenes and many details.

The dream takes place in the front yard of my mother's house. My mother, my son, and I—three generations—are walking through the front yard together, and we see a lawnmower. It's the large riding lawnmower which my son usually uses to mow my mother's extensive property. But hers is green and this one is red, and there's no one controlling it. As we watch, we see that it's going absolutely rampant: it's totally out of control, bouncing off of trees and making loop-de-loops. Suddenly it begins to chase us around the large front yard. My mother begins to scream, "Who has the control? Who has the control?" I answer, "It's a remote control and it's lost, no one has it. No one has the control." In the distance, we see a rose trellis, one of those arched rose trellises like those used at weddings. Hanging from the rose trellis by their horns are two dead, bloated, stinking cows.

Pat woke up from this dream feeling confusion, concern, and disgust. As soon as she got past the unpleasantness, she reached for her journal and wrote down the dream as we've presented it.

It is important to write down as many details as you can remember right away with as little analytical thought as possible. The idea is to work with the initial impressions you have of the dream. When Pat wrote about the lawnmower, she could have said, "no one was riding it" or "it didn't have a driver." Instead she said "...there's no one controlling it." There are connotations connected with the word "control" that are important in understanding the dream. They could be lost if she stopped to think about it or chose another phrase because she thought it might be clearer to someone reading or hearing about the dream.

Next, the emotions that Pat felt as she awoke from the dream should be recorded. In this case the emotions were strong—confusion, concern, and disgust—and they were combined with an equally vivid memory of the smell of the dead cows. This information will help to focus interpretations later, so we must capture it as soon as possible. Oftentimes, as we said in Chapter 2, when we don't remember a dream, we do remember the feeling we awoke with, and that in itself can provide some guidance or help for us.

Finally, Pat needed to establish some background. To do this, she looked at the events of the last few days. For several weeks, she had been involved in planning a wedding for the son who appeared in her dream. The wedding was to take place outdoors, in the very yard which was being mowed so wildly in the dream, with the main part of the ceremony to be held under the rose arbor. As stress is not uncommon before weddings, while Pat and her mother were working out the logistics, her son and his fiancée were getting more and more nervous about the whole thing. There was no obvious mention of the wedding in the dream, but it was probable that a connection would be found.

This, then, is the information needed to begin work on the dream: a brief synopsis of the dream, using the language that came most easily and quickly to mind; a quick notation of the waking emotions and impressions; and a short description of what was important in the dreamer's life during the period preceding the dream. Once this information is in place, interpretation can begin.

The easiest way to begin interpretation is to look at the dream to discover what is unusual, out-of-place, unique, or different in it.

UNUSUAL ELEMENTS IN PAT'S DREAM:

Lawnmower:

- *No one is controlling it and it's running wild, making a mess of the yard.*

- *It has a missing remote control in the dream (it is not normally operated by remote control).*

- *It's red, where it's normally green.*

Rose arbor:

- *There are dead cows hanging from the rose arbor.*

- *The smell of the cows was very strong, clearly to ensure that Pat notices them.*

The reason for looking at these details first is that they are the ones that the unconscious is "pointing to." The unconscious says, "OK, here's a common setting, people you know (or people who are like people you know). Now look over here at *this*." And "*this*" will be an exaggerated detail, or something missing, or something in a different color than it normally is, or something/someone behaving in a most unusual way. This is how the unconscious draws your attention to the important aspects of the dream it has created for you.

Next, Pat examined direct questions and answers, as well as strong statements, especially if they were repeated. Pat remembered a clear question: "Who has the control?" And it is repeated, in case we missed it the first time! The answer is also important: "It's a remote control, and it's lost. No one has the control."

So in the dream, Pat is plopped down in the middle of her mother's beautiful yard, which is to be the setting for the wedding that everyone's been so wrapped up in—and the yard is being absolutely ruined by this out-of-control and uncontrolled lawnmower. "Who usually sits in this lawnmower? Who usually *controls* it?" Pat asked herself. The answer was her son, but the dream, with its direct question and answer, made it clear that no one was controlling the machine any longer. Moreover, the machine was now bright red, rather than its usual green.

This son was their youngest, shyest, and most sensitive child, and he had not spoken a word to her about how he was feeling. Yet, by paying attention to the lawnmower's action and change of color from green to red, Pat began to see that her son was close to losing even "the remotest control" over his emotions. What should be a happy occasion was causing him great frustration and anger.

The grandmother was also upset in the dream, but she did not hide it. She was concerned about the appearance of the yard, which was being ruined by this out-of-control machine. This was the first wedding of a grandchild and was to be held on her property, in a beautiful garden setting. The dream showed Pat that the whole event had become a spectacle-in-the-making, rather than the simple, beautiful affair which everyone had intended it to be.

But what about those dead cows? They were still a mystery to Pat. So she used an old trick from psychology: association. What came to mind if she began to let her mind float around the concept of "cow"? "Lazy cow," "fat cow," "mother cow," "milk," "nurturing,"—none of these seemed to ring any bells. They were close, perhaps, but there was no "Bingo!" yet. But then, suddenly (along with that little "Aha!" feeling, a sure sign that she was getting warm), into her mind came the idea of "sacred cows."

To Pat, "sacred cows" signified long-held religious beliefs which were not much use to anyone anymore but which still had to be honored and respected. We need to stress here that it doesn't matter whether or not Pat's understanding of a "sacred cow" is correct; all that matters at this point is what the concept or word or idea means for her. It is *her understanding* of "sacred cow" which the unconscious used when it was putting together the dream. Once she had made the "sacred cow" connection, Pat could see that the dead cows symbolized some of her mother's deeply held religious and social beliefs. The dream vividly demonstrated what was happening to these beliefs. They were being slaughtered and would be hung out for all to see, stinking and swollen, if things continued as they were going.

All this was making sense; but Pat still needed to know what the sacred cows actually represented, what long-standing beliefs would be publicly destroyed if, for example, the wedding plans were abandoned and the couple eloped? Simple: Pat and her mother were Catholic, and for both of them a civil ceremony would not be satisfactory, not to mention the social embarrassment of making all these arrangements and then having to tell friends and relatives that there would be no wedding.

Intuitively and unconsciously, Pat had known that her son was upset, though his natural shyness had not let him share his feelings with her. She had also known how important the wedding was to her mother. But through the dream Pat was able to see several important things that she had not seen clearly before on a conscious level. She saw her son's predicament, how close he was to losing control, to running away. She saw what this would do to the beautiful wedding everyone was planning. And lastly she saw how her mother would react if the wedding plans failed.

Through the dream, Pat's higher consciousness had given her some very valuable assistance. It was a signal that she should sit down first with her son and then with her mother and let the emotions each of them had been hiding come out. And she herself had a much clearer idea now of their respective positions, so that she could help to bring forth this necessary communication before the situation got out of hand.

Let's review the steps that Pat followed in order to understand this dream. First of all, she wrote down the dream, quickly, giving her first impressions. Then she noted what she had been working on in her life the day before she had the dream. She also listed the emotions and strong feelings she had when she woke up from the dream.

She then searched through the dream to find the elements that were out of the ordinary. She noted the questions and responses that were obvious in the dream. Finally, she looked at people, actions, colors, and feelings associated with objects in the dream, and at her own emotions, in order to determine how they were being used as symbols in the dream. With all of this information and analysis under her belt, she was able to extract the message in the dream.

As a postscript, it's interesting to know how Pat used the dream to handle this situation. She went to her son, told him the dream, and simply said: "If this is really the case, if you are really thinking of eloping secretly and you can't talk about it, just raise your hand. If you don't raise your hand, I'll know that it's anxiety on my part and that I just need to deal with my own feelings."

The young man burst out, "Oh, Mom, you and your dumb dreams!" —but as Pat watched, he silently raised his hand. Disaster was avoided, another plan was developed that was agreeable to all, and the wedding went off without a hitch (no pun intended).

Now, let's see how all of this might look if it appeared in a dream journal. We have reproduced the format of two pages from the dream journal portion of this workbook. We have written in the information and notes about the remote-controlled lawnmower dream that Pat might have made if she had had a journal like this one at the time.

Following Pat's dream, we present a second dream using the journal format again. All of the information the dreamer has upon waking has been filled in on the left-hand journal page. We'll discuss this second dream and how the meaning was reached, just to be sure the process is clear, and then we'll fill in the right-hand journal page.

Whatever you dream you can do, begin it.
Boldness has genius, power and magic in it.
Begin it now.

Johann W. Von Goethe

DATE: 9/12/86

GUIDANCE QUESTION: None

WAKING EMOTIONS: Confusion, concern, disgust; strong stench of dead cows.

DREAM TITLE: Remote-Controlled Lawnmower

DREAM: The dream takes place in the front yard of my mother's house. My mother, my son, and I--three generations--are walking through the front yard together, and we see a lawnmower. It's the large riding lawnmower which my son usually uses to mow my mother's extensive property. But hers is green and this one is red, and there's no one controlling it. As we watch, we see that it's totally out of control, bouncing off of trees and making loop-de-loops. Suddenly it begins to chase us around the large front yard. My mother begins to scream, "Who has the control? Who has the control?" And I answer, "It's a remote control and it's lost, no one has it. No one has the control." In the distance, we see a rose trellis, one of those arched rose trellises like those used at weddings. Hanging from the rose trellis by their horns are two dead, bloated, stinking cows.

RECENT CONCERNS: Preparations for my son's wedding. Mother getting more and more excited; son seeming more and more frustrated.

SETTING: Mother's yard

UNUSUAL DETAILS: Lawnmower: No one is controlling it and it's running wild, making a mess of the yard. It has a missing remote control. It's red, where it's normally green. Rose arbor: There are dead cows hanging from the rose arbor. The smell of the cows is very strong.

STATEMENTS/QUESTIONS/ANSWERS: "Who has the control?" This is repeated. Answer to the question: "It's a remote control and it's lost, no one has it. No one has the control."

SYMBOLS AT WORK: Yard: surrounds house, acts here as a symbol of mother and her emotional peace. Red lawnmower: out of control; seems to be representing my son's emotions. Dead sacred cows: represent the beliefs of mother, both religious and social, which would be "slaughtered" if things continue to be out of control.

DREAM MESSAGE: My mother is very concerned from a religious and social standpoint that this wedding be properly carried out--more concerned than I realized. Similarly, my son is much more frustrated than I knew, and he is very likely to go out of control--possibly elope--if something isn't done. I need to talk to both of them about these fears and emotions.

DATE: 6/18/91

GUIDANCE QUESTION: None

WAKING EMOTIONS: Fright; concern that I should go to the dentist.

DREAM TITLE: Teeth Falling Out

DREAM: I'm in front of the mirror brushing my teeth to clean them, and I
notice that they are loose. So I touch my tongue to my teeth, and, as I do,
my teeth begin to fall out. Some of them break, some of them drop out whole.
I hold my hand under my mouth, and they drop into my hand.

RECENT CONCERNS: Angry with Carol at the office; called Alice to let off
steam. Someone backed into my car and scratched the door.

OK, let's stop here before continuing with the journal format. It's the next morning, and our dreamer has written out her short dream on the left-hand dream journal page. This dream did not come in response to a request for guidance (we'll work with that a little bit later). Nevertheless, if it isn't already obvious that the dream offers some guidance, it soon will be clear. Remember, *all dreams are guidance dreams.*

The dream is written down completely here, as it first occurred to the dreamer. Of course, if she had been in a hurry when she woke up, she could just have written a title for the dream. This title would contain enough of a clue to bring the details back to her mind later when she had more time to write the dream down. In addition to a title, we hope she would also have written down her emotions upon waking. These two elements, a title and the emotional response to the dream, provide the most valuable assistance when we need to come back later to remember our earlier dreams.

There are two things we should point out about this journal page. First, the dreamer has underlined an action in the dream which *she* feels is especially significant (if this were a longer dream, there might be two or three of these underlined actions). This is an action which she feels is especially important. Someone else reading or working with the dream might have a different sense of the most important elements, but it is the *dreamer's* sense of what is significant that is valuable here. Underlining will help her to see where the dream is focused.

Secondly, many people have lengthy, involved dreams, which fill several pages. Such dreams can usually be broken down into scenes, sort of like a multi-act play. We suggest that you treat each of these scenes as a separate section in your journal. Use pages for each section, but then note that the sections are all part of the same dream (You might add (A), (B), (C), and so on after the title.) After dealing separately with each of the parts, go back and find the common symbols or ideas that occur in some or all of the parts. These would constitute the basic message of the entire dream.

For example, Pat Shepherd's daughter Karen dreamed a "five-act" dream not too long ago. When Pat Fregia worked with her on the dream, they found that four of the acts served as a sort of review of stages in Karen's life. Each was complete in itself and could be worked with separately. The fifth act summarized the others and showed how, in each of these stages, she had been seeking to understand who she was and what she was supposed to do with her life. This act, too, could be analyzed by itself. But a much more important message was derived when the five-part structure of the dream was understood.

But let's return to our dream of teeth falling out. At the right, now, we have the right-hand page of the journal entry for this dream. Let's look at how our dreamer used the page to see what the dream was telling her. She has written in the setting, and she has noted the unusual details. It's not impossible for teeth to fall out, but the dreamer's teeth are in good shape, and it would be very unusual for this to suddenly occur.

There were no statements or questions in the dream, so the next step is to work with the other two elements. She looks first at the setting and what it represents. The bathroom is generally a place of cleansing. Usually there is a mirror, in which we can see ourselves. What is being cleaned in front of this mirror? Teeth. Where do we normally find teeth? In our mouths. What else is significant about the mouth? The mouth and tongue are used for speech.

When our dreamer reached this point, she could stop and assess what she had learned. She is in the bathroom, a place of cleansing. As she touches her tongue to her teeth, they fall out. To put it another way, when she uses her tongue, something destructive takes place: she becomes less attractive to herself and others. "Aha!" She can now make the connection (if she's not in denial) between teeth—objects that we find in the mouth—and words, which are produced by the mouth. From here, she deduces that some of her words may be destructive to herself and others.

To recap: The dreamer finds herself in the bathroom literally facing herself. She sees that her tongue has gotten her in trouble, and because of it, her true beauty has been diminished.

"Aha! Aha! I've got it," says our dreamer. Because of her bad feelings toward Carol, and the complaints she voiced to Alice—and possibly also because of some pretty unattractive things that she had to say about that careless driver!—she has received a little scolding/warning from her higher self. To wit: "When you gossip or speak negatively about others, you are really defacing yourself. You need to rid yourself of this habit."

SETTING: Bathroom, in front of mirror.

UNUSUAL DETAILS: Teeth: They're loose, falling out. Some are whole, some are broken.

STATEMENTS/QUESTIONS/ANSWERS: None.

SYMBOLS AT WORK: Bathroom: place of cleansing. Mirror: self is reflected in it; look at self. Tongue: means of speech. Loose teeth: words coming from mouth used carelessly. Broken teeth: destructive words falling from mouth, leaving jagged edges, ugly gaps.

DREAM MESSAGE: Because of my anger at Carol, my running to Alice to complain about it, and the ugly things I said about that driver who scratched my car, I've been "scolded" in my dream. It's telling me that talk like that really defaces me, makes me appear ugly. I really should try to rid myself of this habit.

She has not only received a gentle lesson, but she has acquired some new first-hand experience with several symbols which will be helpful as she works through future dreams.

This dream easily classifies as a personal development/self-awareness dream. It vividly shows how destructive gossip can be, both to others, and especially to ourselves and to our values. Our dreamer was reminded that, by the use of her tongue and her mouth, she was breaking things, causing damage to herself, to her appearance, and to her self-esteem. This is a very simple dream, but many simple dreams are frequently misunderstood. (Remember our dreamer's initial reaction: "I'd better get to a dentist right away.")

DREAM ALERT

It's important to see that our higher selves can counsel us in a number of situations. For example, we might find ourselves in front of a mirror combing our hair, which is all tangled and matted, or which is even a different color than normal. Here again we are being directed to see that something needs to be changed or straightened up or smoothed out or cleansed. When we deal with aspects of our appearance such as dress, shoes, hair, or teeth, we can be fairly certain we are being asked to look at and change some aspect of our attitudes or beliefs.

Now, let's look at a dream that came as the result of a request for guidance. Tom was considering the purchase of a business which he would be running in partnership with a good friend. He had worked through all the financial details and was pretty close to a decision. But before he committed himself, he decided to ask for input from his higher self. So, following the steps given in Chapter 2, he wrote down his question on a piece of paper and, literally, slept on it. On the next two pages, we present the dream he received and the journal work he did on it.

Tom asked for guidance, phrasing his question, "Should I buy this business?" so that it could be answered either "yes" or "no." Questions like this one are the best kind to ask the unconscious. We advise against asking long questions or questions that include several parts. This is simply because, as we've seen, the unconscious does not always present messages that are easy to understand. It makes sense, in return, not to present it with questions that could have complex answers.

Let's begin with the setting. The dream takes place on a highway, which usually represents our life path. Tom is asking a question about the path his life should take, so this setting signals that we will be getting an answer. A van, like a pick-up truck or tractor, can often have connotations of work; this is reinforced here by the presence of the business logo on the side of the van. So we can assume that the dream is revealing how the business would work out in Tom's life.

The unusual details are, in some cases, not too hard to figure out: the partner as a clown shows us that Tom's unconscious wants him to see that this person is not a serious businessman. Yet Tom is aware that this business is nothing to "clown around" with. Next, Tom's son appears in the dream younger than he is in real life. It doesn't make sense to think that the dream is telling Tom about some earlier moment when the son was in danger, perhaps nearly killed by being run over. There's no way that such a message would be helpful to Tom. For that reason, we need to look at the son in a different way.

Tom has written that his son symbolizes, "My younger, naive, childlike, less mature side." To understand this, we need another lesson in dream interpretation, which appears as a *Dream Alert* on page 86. In real life, Tom's son is young, but, in his dream, the boy is younger than usual. By having the child younger than in reality (an exaggerated or unusual detail), even more emphasis is placed on youth and immaturity. So Tom is absolutely correct in assuming that the boy represents these aspects of himself.

DATE: 10/23/87

GUIDANCE QUESTION: Should I buy this business?

WAKING EMOTIONS: Anxiety

DREAM TITLE: Clown Driving Van

DREAM: I see a white, van-like truck driving down the highway; on its side is the logo of the business I am considering investing in. I recognize the driver of the truck as the man who will be my partner; he is dressed in a clown's outfit, with a clown's face, the big red nose and all. Suddenly, my son (who is younger here than he is in real life) runs in front of the truck and is caught under its wheels, but he is not hurt. The truck stops; my son gets up, gets in the truck, and takes over as the truck driver. As the dream ends, I realize that the name of the man in the clown suit, my potential partner, is "Doug Sump."

RECENT CONCERNS: I'm pretty sure about this business I want to buy, but a part of me still has some questions.

SETTING: The highway.

UNUSUAL DETAILS: Partner is seen as clown. Son is younger than he really is. Child is run over but not hurt. Son is driving the van. Partner's name is "Doug Sump," not his real name.

STATEMENTS/QUESTIONS/ANSWERS: None.

SYMBOLS AT WORK: Highway: road or path the dreamer is traveling along. Van: work vehicle, related to the business (especially with the business's logo on its side). Clown: funny, silly person, not one to be taken seriously. Son: my younger, naive, child-like, less mature side. "Doug Sump": play on words--literally, "dug a cesspool."

DREAM MESSAGE: I should not buy this business. My partner is not serious about things; the business would literally run over the child-like side of me. I would wind up having to take control of things, and I'm not ready to do that yet. In other words, if I bought this business, I would wind up in a stinking hole.

DREAM ALERT

Whenever a person from our life (alive, dead, known personally, or familiar from the media) appears in our dreams, we should initially assume the character represents some aspect of ourselves. To understand just what the person represents, list three attributes or qualities that come quickly to mind when we think about that person. (Psychologists often use this tool, called "association.") This list indicates the characteristics that the unconscious can represent in our dreams by using that person.

Let's look at an example. For Aunt Mabel, we would offer these three attributes or characteristics: she's comfortably plump, her home is filled with old, worn, but comfortable furniture, and she's always knitting sweaters. These are the things that first come to mind when we think of her. Of course, she's many other things, and someone else—Uncle Bob, for example, who has been married to her for 38 years and still sees her as the flirty, blue-eyed, slim-waisted girl he first noticed in the school library—might not even recognize her from our list.

But that's unimportant. What matters is that, if Aunt Mabel showed up in one of our dreams, our unconscious would add the comforting and nurturing feelings we connect with her to the dream situation. If she were present in one of Uncle Bob's dreams, his unconscious might be stressing the youthful, romantic aspects of his feelings about her. She would serve different functions for different dreamers, depending on how the dreamer saw her in "real" life.

Remember, our dreams most often give us knowledge about ourselves rather than about anyone else, unless we absolutely cannot find a message for ourself in the dream. So once we've decided what Aunt Mabel represents for us, we must see how those characteristics belong to—or should belong to—us. To show us we've become too cold and uncaring, the unconscious looks through its catalog of characteristics, finds Aunt Mabel listed under "warm and nurturing," and, that night, presents Aunt Mabel knocking at the door to an empty deserted house. We need to open the door and let the ability to be warm and nurturing come into our life.

Once we see this, we need to ask what qualities are being brought to Tom's attention: one would seem to be his idealistic naïveté about the financial potential of this business. With this in mind, let's go back to the dream and see what happens to this youth. First of all, he gets run over by the van (in other words, by the business), driven by the clown (partner). Then, Tom must take over the wheel and assume control—and the dream shows us that he is clearly not ready (as symbolized by the young son) to take control at this point. In other words, if he takes on the business, he's got a clown for a partner; he would then most likely have to take over the entire business himself, and he's not ready.

This is a dream with a message that is really hard to miss. The dream indicates that Tom will wind up in a stinking hole ("Doug Sump") if he buys the business. Even if he had not remembered the entire dream, the emotion of anxiety with which he awoke gave Tom his answer. There was nothing comfortable about it; the answer was "NO!"

Great! You're on a roll. Now, let's work through some more dreams. On the following two pages, we present another interesting dream that takes us in a different direction. Again, let's assume the dreamer has filled in the left-hand page with the information which can be found by just looking at the dream. She has done this either when she awoke from the dream or at some later time. The right-hand page presents the analysis of the dream. Read the left-hand page and then try to anticipate what we've put down on the right-hand page as practice for your own dreamwork.

DATE: 9/26/89

GUIDANCE QUESTION: None

WAKING EMOTIONS: Fear for my child, strong need to protect him.

DREAM TITLE: Bees and Tinfoil

DREAM: I'm in my house, and it's a very warm, cozy, nice house, and my two-year-old child is playing. All of a sudden, there's a swarm of bees inside the house. I ask my mother and my sister to take the child upstairs and wrap him in tinfoil to cover him and protect him so the bees won't sting him. At first, I think I can get rid of the bees myself, but I can't. I become more and more alarmed, and I realize, finally, I am going to have to call a professional exterminator to get rid of the bees. That was the end of the dream.

RECENT CONCERNS: All the problems between my husband and me, which just seem to be getting worse every day.

SETTING: Nice cozy home.

UNUSUAL DETAILS: Swarm of bees in house. Mother and sister present in my

house. Wrapping child in tinfoil.

STATEMENTS/QUESTIONS/ANSWERS: None.

SYMBOLS AT WORK: Cozy home: represents family situation; security. Swarm

of bees: the possibility of lots of little aggravations, stings, pains.

Professional exterminator: someone, not me, trained and hired to do a job that

needs to be done. Mother: nurturing, caring, protecting side of me. Sister:

social worker; realistic; friend. Tinfoil: a kind of protection, armor,

shield against ills.

DREAM MESSAGE: All the little petty annoyances that have been accumulating in

my home recently have the potential to harm my child. I've been thinking that

I could protect him but this shows me I can't. I really need to get some

professional help in this situation.

As usual, the place to begin is with the first sentence and the setting it establishes for us. In this dream, the setting is the home, a warm comfortable place in which a child is happily playing, and all appears to be normal. But this normal situation is upset and interrupted by the swarm of bees, which shows up inside the house. The dreamer has noted that this is not a usual place to find a swarm of bees.

Therefore, she knows she must look carefully at the swarm of bees, to see what they represent. Whatever they represent is upsetting her cozy home situation. Usually, an insect represents some small annoyance, and for most people this would be the case with a bee. (Note, however, that if you are one of those people for whom a single bee sting can be fatal, a bee might mean something considerably different.) But here we have a whole swarm of bees, lots of potential stings, which can present a serious threat to anyone, especially a small child. So the dreamer notes that the bees represent a collection, a swarm, of the small annoyances that seem to be going on in her home, which, one at a time, would be no problem but which, in a swarm, are clearly capable of causing serious harm.

Looking back at the dream, we see that the dreamer's first thought is for the child (she has underlined the words that involve protecting him). She asks the mother and sister to help her protect him.

Her mother and sister, who are not normally in her home, need to be seen as parts of herself; she has given attributes for them on the right-hand journal page. The mother here is just that—the mothering side of her. The sister is not quite as obvious. Here's how Pat explains it: "It's a lot easier for us to openly and honestly criticize or praise our sister—or brother, as the case may be—than ourselves, so a sister or brother often shows up in our dreams as a stand-in for ourself." By listing attributes for the mother and sister, the dreamer sees that the realistic, practical, mothering side of herself in the dream has the job of protecting the child.

The mother and sister encase the child in a kind of armor (tinfoil in the dream). Though this might, in fact, protect the child from actual bee stings, it wouldn't be a very comfortable or efficient way for him to live. In other words, the protection she can provide will not be enough to allow him to function effectively in his world. The bees are a real threat to her child, and she must get rid of them altogether.

But she can't do it by herself, no matter how strong her mothering instincts are: she must finally call a professional exterminator to get rid of the bees. She must seek trained, professional help outside of herself.

When we translate this message to her real-life situation, we can see clearly what her dream reveals. She and her husband have been having problems in their relationship, which to this point have been limited to small annoyances, petty bickerings over minor problems. She is aware of this tension but has felt able to handle it and keep it from having any effect on her child.

But the dream shows her that the small annoyances that were present in her home have grown into a situation that may harm her child. She alone, with all the strength and mothering ability she can muster, is not capable of shielding her child from the anger and bitterness that is growing between herself and her husband. Nor does she have the ability to get rid of these harmful attitudes and annoyances that have grown to such dangerous proportions. The dream says very specifically to her: "You cannot solve this problem on your own. Get professional help."

Let's try another one. For this dream, we are going to introduce another technique that is most helpful in dream work. Again, the dream and its "work-through" appear on the next pair of pages. We'd like you to turn to pages 92 and 93, read the dream and the analysis presented there, and then come back here for a discussion of the dream.

A listener, let's call her Linda, phoned in this dream during one of our monthly radio talk show visits. When Linda finished telling us the dream, we asked her what John F. Kennedy meant to her, how she interpreted him. We were asking for the two or three attributes which came to her mind whenever she thought about Kennedy. Her immediate response was, "He was a dashing figure, who was shot down too early."

Now, not everyone would have the same quick response to that question. For some, Kennedy was a modern-day King Arthur; for others, an assassinated hero; for still others he was the great playboy of the western world. Each of us could come up with our own attributes for him, and even if we thought of him in the same way as someone else, we would come up with different ways of describing those attributes. What is important is that a specific attribute appears for each of us to interpret.

DATE: 4/10/90

GUIDANCE QUESTION: None

WAKING EMOTIONS: Confusion.

DREAM TITLE: JFK As Gynecologist

DREAM: I dreamed that John F. Kennedy was my gynecologist. He had written his phone number down on a business card, but it seemed to have been crossed out, and I am trying to get in touch with him. The number was wrong or there was something bad about it.

RECENT CONCERNS: I'm trying to decide whether or not to close down the business which I've been struggling with for so many years. I'm really sad about this. I thought the business would make it.

SETTING: No definite setting.

UNUSUAL DETAILS: President John F. Kennedy as a gynecologist.

Wrong or "bad" numbers.

STATEMENTS/QUESTIONS/ANSWERS: None.

SYMBOLS AT WORK: John F. Kennedy: a dashing figure, shot down too early.

Gynecologist: medical professional, usually involved in the birth of babies.

Business card: tool of identity from the world of business. Numbers: a

business's "numbers" are sort of like its temperature--they indicate how

the business is doing.

DREAM MESSAGE: My business really is dead (though it has died too soon, just

like John F. Kennedy did). The mishandling of the books killed it, and I'd

better just bury it and go on to something else.

We've established Linda's feelings about President Kennedy: she thought of him as "a dashing figure who had been shot down too early." A gynecologist, of course, is a doctor who deals with the female reproductive organs. So the dream has something to do with birth, or getting started. The business card is a tool of the business world, so perhaps what's getting started is some sort of business.

Putting all of this together, our next question to Linda was, "What exciting business are you 'giving birth to' that is getting off to a bad start, that could be 'shot down' too early?" The business card signaled that the focus was on a new enterprise that, like JFK, showed great potential and would look great but was being assassinated, or prevented from fulfilling its true promise.

The final element to examine in the dream is the "bad numbers." There was something wrong with the business's numbers (the books). This, we felt, was the reason the business had been "shot down" before it got off the ground.

Linda was surprised and told us she had been struggling with a business for several years. She let a relative come in to manage it, but things had not been doing well. An accountant went over the books, but he had not been competent and had gotten the business into some tax problems. She told us she was starting to feel that the only answer was to close down the venture, but she was reluctant to do this, since it seemed to have such promise.

She had been trying to sort things out logically, using her conscious mind. But it took the "logic" of the unconscious to clear things up. For all intents and purposes, the business was dead. While it originally showed great promise, it had been dealt a fatal blow by the mishandling of the books. All of this becomes clear once we understand how Linda's unconscious was using John F. Kennedy here.

Now that we've shown you the workbook technique in action, we're going to send you off on your own to practice with a few dreams. But first, we want to reinforce our earlier discussion about how people are used in dreams. We spend most of our lives dealing with people and relationships. So people provide the basic building blocks for most of our dreams.

These can be people we are close to, people we are only slightly acquainted with, people we love, people we can't stand, relatives, people from another planet, the rich and famous, the notorious and infamous, sick people, healthy people,

people who have passed away, and even people whose faces we can't see and whom we may or may not know.

As we have said, finding an attribute for a person or people who appear in your dreams is a wonderfully effective technique for learning a dream's message. It's used by most people who work with dreams, as we do. We know that ninety percent of the time our dreams are about us. But we are not always ready to hear things about ourselves in flat-out declarative statements, so our unconscious pulls other people into our dreams to serve as illustrations or representations of those points it wants us to understand. Our unconscious knows how we feel about the people in our lives and uses that knowledge to carefully pick out those people who exhibit or incorporate the particular trait we are supposed to pay attention to in ourselves.

Moreover, we might come up with different attributes for people on different days. For example, Denise could have a dream in which her brother, Alan, appears. Now, if Denise had just had a run-in with Alan the day before the dream, when we ask for an attribute she might respond with, "Impatient bully." But if the dream occurs during the night after Alan has come over, unasked, to pull all the leaves out of Denise's stopped-up gutters, she might give "sensitive and caring" as her attributes for him. Either answer is appropriate if it's what comes to Denise's mind when she thinks of Alan. And whatever she says will be most helpful in understanding the message of the dream in which Alan appeared.

Thus, if Denise has been pretty impatient lately, wanting her life to take a particular direction that just doesn't seem to be happening, brother Alan (remember, the one she just had a misunderstanding with?) might show up in her dream. When she pulls that dream apart the next morning, she would list Alan under "Symbols at Work" and quickly write down, "Impatient bully" to indicate how she's seeing Alan *at that moment*. Then, as she examines the dream, she may be able to see that Alan is illustrating an aspect of her own behavior which needs to be examined.

On the other hand, a few days later, when Denise is feeling particularly unsuccessful and unlovable, her unconscious might want to show her that she's really not as undesirable as she thinks. So who would show up in that night's dream? Right, that same brother Alan (this is the day *after* he took care of her gutters for her), only now she is thinking of him fondly as one of the most sensitive and caring people she knows.

When she looks at this second dream the next morning, an entirely different Alan shows up—but again, Denise notes what he represents for her *at that point* and sees that this characteristic belongs to her, too. In both cases, we need to give Alan the attributes we find uppermost in our mind, and then we need to see that the dream wants us to relate that characteristic to ourselves.

There's bad news and there's good news, here. The bad news is that it takes a lot of practice to be able to do all of this objectively, never mind doing it all quickly. Finding attributes for people we hardly know can be a challenge, but it is often even harder to find attributes for people we know well and are very close to. Then we must be objective in examining these attributes to see how they reflect back on us. This requires an openness and vulnerability that is difficult for many.

The good news is that the unconscious will frequently help us by picking people from our lives for whom the particular characteristic is exaggerated. To illustrate unselfishness and devotion to others, we might see Mother Theresa walking along a circus tightrope. If we need to stop being nosy, Jimmy Durante might appear, just in time to have his nose shut in the car door.

As we said, about ninety percent of the time our dreams use other people to give us messages about ourselves. So how can we distinguish the other ten percent, those relatively rare dreams which are about someone else, someone for whom we are being asked to provide some form of assistance? The rule of thumb is to first work on any dream with the assumption that it has a message for you. Look for attributes for the people in the dream, find and examine its unusual details, try to understand the symbolism it is using, and work at the dream until you feel that "Aha!" If you do all of these things, however, and that "Aha!" just doesn't seem to be there, *then* you might begin to look at the dream as being about someone else. Let's look at an example.

One night, a number of years ago now, Pat had a dream about her friend Dottie:

> *Dottie was skating on ice and doing a beautiful job of it. She was pirouetting and spinning, and she looked very impressive. She was*

dressed in a ballerina's tutu, and, as I watched her skate, I could see that there was a big hot cross bun (the kind with an X in frosting on it) right on Dottie's rear end.

Pat remembers vividly that she awoke with the impression that Dottie had skated "just like Sonja Henie." Sonja Henie was a famous skater who had won a number of Olympic medals in the 1930s and had also appeared in several popular movies of the day. Pat had always been impressed with her abilities, and as she woke up and began to remember the dream, those words stuck with her: "Dottie was skating just like Sonja Henie."

She went to work right away on the dream, asking herself the question "What are my attributes for Dottie?" Dottie was blonde, a dear friend, and had a lot of physical problems. Okay, Pat said, how do these apply to me? Well, Pat, too, is blonde, and she felt about herself—as we all should—that she was her own best friend. So that left the physical problems: what physical problem did she, Pat, have that she might be skating around? Or, perhaps she was skating on thin ice regarding something.

Well, try as she might, she just couldn't find one. And that hot cross bun was a real puzzler. She remembered the nursery rhyme, "One-a-penny, two-a-penny, hot cross bun," but she couldn't see anything significant about it. All in all, there was definitely no "Aha!"

At this point, she took the next step. When she was sure she could not find any way to relate the dream to herself, she called the person who appeared in the dream. "Dottie," she said, "let me tell you my dream. You were skating beautifully, like Sonja Henie, but you had this big hot-cross-bun on your rear end."

There was a pause. Then Dottie said, "Well, Pat, you've done it again. My deepest desire—and no one ever knew this—was to be an ice skater."

"Neat," said Pat, "and you were doing it beautifully. But why did you have the hot cross bun on your rear end? And what are you skating around or skating on thin ice about?"

"Well, I didn't want to have to tell anyone about this, but I've had a sore on my tailbone for some time now. I've been hoping it would just go away, but it doesn't seem to want to do that."

"Aha!" Pat heard it loud and clear. "Dottie," she said, "this message that I got in my dream is for you because you've been blocking it in *your* dreams. You need to have that sore tended to. It's hot (cross bun) and you're skating on thin ice. Get yourself to the doctor and have him look at that thing on your hiney." And that's when it hit Pat: "Sonja Henie = It's onya hiney."

There were several clues to help Dottie get the message in this dream: the bun (on her "buns") with the "X" marking the spot, the fact that the bun was a hot cross bun, and that wonderful pun on the name Sonja Henie. A couple of postscripts need to be added here. One of the reasons the pun worked for Pat is that, while most of the world says "henny" when they see that skater's name, Pat says "hiney." Also, when Dottie did get to the doctor, it was found that the growth was very troublesome and needed to be removed right away.

Here we have a classic situation where, because of fear that her sore might be a serious problem, Dottie just wasn't ready to hear consciously some very important information. So Pat was given the information (Jung would say this was the universal unconscious doing its thing). Pat was very close to Dottie, cared very much about her, and was someone who could receive and relay the message that Dottie needed.

Now, we've discussed how to look for the unusual details, the significant actions, the symbols and the attributes of the objects, people, and events in your dreams. One other point needs to be stressed again: whatever words you use to tell about your dreams are the right words. It's very important that you write down your dreams as soon as you can, without worrying too much about grammar or vocabulary. And when you tell someone else your dream, instruct the listener to let you stumble around and find your own words to describe the events, the people, or the objects in your dreams.

There is an obvious reason for this: your unconscious is never asleep. As we have seen, it works hard even when you are not conscious. But it is just as busy when you are conscious, and it is there helping you find ways to say things. So if you blurt out, "The lady was puny," and your listener says, "You mean, petite?" "No," you must answer, sticking to your guns, "puny, P-U-N-Y." And at that moment, you realize that you've hit on something: "P-U," stinky, smelly—which you might never have come upon if you'd gone along with your listener's suggestion of "petite."

Or, as you describe a dream in which a church appears, you very specifically call it a "Presbyterian" church. Three times, as you relate the details of the dream, you find yourself using that same adjective, "Presbyterian," to describe this building. Your unconscious *wants* you to notice that word—take the suggestion, and consult a good dictionary as you are working through the dream. Look up the word, even if you think you know what it means; look at all of the meanings that are offered, and see if one or another of them triggers that "Aha!" We found ourselves in just that situation: "Presbyterian" came up several times as we worked with someone on a dream. We know that Presbyterianism is one branch of the Protestant religion, but this didn't help us until we finally went to the dictionary to find that the word actually means "council of elders." Aha! Here was just the clue we needed to open up this dream. We simply needed to listen to our unconscious as it urged us to pay attention to a particular detail.

Open your intuition to the part of you which knows. Decisions made by cold reason alone are made to satisfy others. An intuitive decision needs to satisfy only you; it doesn't matter if others think you are crazy. When you become authentic, you are no longer concerned with what others think. Have faith in yourself and your Master Teacher.

Enough teaching—it's time to practice. We'll provide six dreams with the information you need to work through the dreams. Try reading the dream over, underlining the action words in the dream which seem most important, and then filling in the blanks on the right-hand journal page.

Do as much of this on your own as you can; when you feel you've finished— or at least done all you can—turn to the pages that follow these six dreams, and you'll find our discussions of each one (identified by the title we've given on the dream journal page). Remember, there are no right answers here. What strikes you as important in your dreams *is* what's important. (Of course, these are not your dreams, but the principle still holds.)

DATE: 4/17/87

GUIDANCE QUESTION: Why am I so unhappy?

WAKING EMOTIONS: Fear about walking around bald.

DREAM TITLE: Scalping

DREAM: I dreamed I was sitting in a barber's chair, and the barber was giving me a haircut. I could see the hair falling all over the floor. The barber kept cutting until my scalp was bare, and then he began to cut my eyebrows, until he had cut all the hair off my eyebrows. I was feeling very anxious as I sat there and looked down at all the hair on the floor.

RECENT CONCERNS: I'm not sure I'm in the right profession. Seems as though, if I were, things would be going a lot better for me than they are.

SETTING: _____

UNUSUAL DETAILS: _____

_____

_____

_____

STATEMENTS/QUESTIONS/ANSWERS: _____

_____

_____

SYMBOLS AT WORK: _____

_____

_____

_____

_____

_____

_____

DREAM MESSAGE: _____

_____

_____

_____

_____

_____

DATE: 2/12/90

GUIDANCE QUESTION: None.

WAKING EMOTIONS: Very anxious; my stomach was upset.

DREAM TITLE: Throwing Cactus

DREAM: I was walking through the woods with this guy, talking about things I needed to do to clear up some problems in my life. He said, "But it is so important that we do this right." As we walked along, I suddenly saw this fence that was about 12 to 18 feet high, bent over with barbed wire at the top. There were these three huge, round-shaped cactuses. The guy said that we had to dig them up and throw them over the other side of the fence so that they would hit the ground without breaking. We had to beware of the thorns. He dug up the first two, and they hit the ground without breaking. But when I dug up the third one and threw it over the fence, it burst when it hit the ground, releasing a bunch of water. When I looked at it, I was so emotional because it had burst. When I woke up, I was emotional. I remember I didn't eat for two or three days.

RECENT CONCERNS: Should I move out of my parent's house into my own apartment? I'm also concerned about the constant state of conflict I have with my family.

SETTING: _____

UNUSUAL DETAILS: _____

_____

_____

_____

STATEMENTS/QUESTIONS/ANSWERS: _____

_____

_____

SYMBOLS AT WORK: _____

_____

_____

_____

_____

_____

_____

DREAM MESSAGE: _____

_____

_____

_____

_____

_____

DATE: 5/21/91

GUIDANCE QUESTION: None.

WAKING EMOTIONS: Great! I must be doing something right!

DREAM TITLE: 1-4-3

DREAM: I walk into a Catholic cathedral and go to a pew. As I am kneeling in the pew, I see a statue of Christ in the front of the church, behind glass. He has one hand raised, not really high but just up in the air. There are a number of other people in the church, but as I look at this statue, I can see it is looking at me. Then I see that it is motioning with its raised arm. As I look, I see the statue hold up one finger, then close its hand, then hold up four fingers, then close its hand, then hold up three fingers, then close its hand. I know it's a miracle that I'm seeing, and I take my camera up there, because I want to get a picture of it so that other people can see it.

RECENT CONCERNS: Am I doing the right thing, going in the right direction?

SETTING: _____

UNUSUAL DETAILS: _____

_____

_____

_____

STATEMENTS/QUESTIONS/ANSWERS: _____

_____

_____

SYMBOLS AT WORK: _____

_____

_____

_____

_____

_____

_____

DREAM MESSAGE: _____

_____

_____

_____

_____

_____

DATE: 1/15/92

GUIDANCE QUESTION: None.

WAKING EMOTIONS: Confusion.

DREAM TITLE: The Urinal

DREAM: I walk into the men's bathroom and stand in front of the urinal. While I am relieving myself, I see my wife walk in. She stands beside me in front of the urinal, and she too begins to relieve herself in exactly the same way as I do--with the same equipment.

RECENT CONCERNS: When am I going to find another job so my wife doesn't have to keep supporting the family?

Setting: _____

Unusual details: _____

_____

_____

_____

Statements/questions/answers: _____

_____

_____

Symbols at work: _____

_____

_____

_____

_____

_____

_____

Dream message: _____

_____

_____

_____

_____

_____

DATE: 10/14/90

GUIDANCE QUESTION: None.

WAKING EMOTIONS: Sadness.

DREAM TITLE: Mother Is an Oyster.

DREAM: I dreamed that my mother is trying to talk to me, but I have great difficulty because she is a very large oyster. And her tongue is like the inside meat of an oyster. And on top of the oyster meat is debris, a large fish hook, and more debris. She keeps trying to talk to me, but she keeps going, "Uhbah, blah, bah, bah."

RECENT CONCERNS: Oh, lots of things. But among them is certainly the way my mother just can't seem to learn to listen to me.

SETTING: _____

UNUSUAL DETAILS: _____

_____

_____

_____

STATEMENTS/QUESTIONS/ANSWERS: _____

_____

_____

SYMBOLS AT WORK: _____

_____

_____

_____

_____

_____

DREAM MESSAGE: _____

_____

_____

_____

_____

_____

DATE: 2/8/85

GUIDANCE QUESTION: None.

WAKING EMOTIONS: Bliss

DREAM TITLE: Jesus at our Party

DREAM: I dreamed we were giving a nice party at our house. We had set a lovely table, with an array of food. Many of our good friends were there, and Jesus was at the party. I took a plate, arranged a variety of food on the plate, and held it in front of me, about chest-high. Across from me was my wife, with two of our sons standing, one on each side. Each of us ate from the plate as if it were communion.

RECENT CONCERNS: Not very much, at this time. The last of six children is a few months away from graduation, and I can see myself with time now to focus on my own work.

SETTING: _____

UNUSUAL DETAILS: _____

_____

_____

_____

STATEMENTS/QUESTIONS/ANSWERS: _____

_____

_____

SYMBOLS AT WORK: _____

_____

_____

_____

_____

_____

DREAM MESSAGE: _____

_____

_____

_____

_____

_____

How did you do? Were you able to pull out some of the unusual details and discover how they were being used as symbols in these dreams? Did you find the various details coming together to present a coherent message to the dreamer? We understand that this is difficult to do under most circumstances, and it is especially tough when you don't know very much about the person's situation.

In some ways, though, that can be helpful. To explain this, Pat says: "When I start to work with someone on a dream, he or she will often begin, 'Let me give you a little background on the situation.' I usually stop them right there, because I don't want to be prejudiced by their judgments about events or people. When I *want* to know how they feel about things—the attributes they give people, for example —I ask. But until that time, I just want to hear the dream. 'Just the facts, ma'am. Just the facts.'"

Let's look at how we interpreted the six dreams. Our discussions are presented below for each dream, using the titles from the dream journal pages.

Scalping

We looked first at the setting. This dream takes place in a barber shop, a place where we pay a professional to cut our hair. Then we looked at the unusual elements of the dream. The barber is removing *all* the hair, even the hair on the eyebrows. Did you find yourself underlining "my scalp was bare" and "all the hair off my eyebrows"? Those are the two actions that struck us as noteworthy.

Next we examined the symbols at work in the dream. Hair, of course, is easy to see, and if you've looked ahead at Chapter 5, which deals with dream symbols, you know that hair usually represents our attitudes or beliefs about things. Hair can be tangled or beautiful or kinky or not its true color—and so can our attitudes and beliefs. In this case, we see that a professional has decided that *all* of this hair must go.

Another similar symbol is the eyebrows, which outline and emphasize the eyes, the seat of vision. Here, too, the actions of the professional are saying that the old must go, to make room for the new—and also to allow for even clearer vision.

So what do we have here? This dreamer has asked his higher consciousness for an answer to the question, "Why am I so unhappy?" What was the answer he received? "Your old beliefs and attitudes need to be completely eradicated, eliminated, and removed with professional help. As well, you need to change your perception, the way you look at things."

This dreamer asked a question from deep pain; he got his answer, although it was not an easy one. The next step is up to him: he can follow his guidance, get help, change his attitudes and perceptions, or stay unhappy.

Throwing Cactus

The setting for the opening scene of this dream is "the woods," which usually means that the dreamer is going through some confusion in his life. The "guy" that he's talking to probably represents himself, since he's not identified in any other way. And confusion is exactly what he is talking about to this person: he says that he has to clear up some things in his life. Also, did you remember to write down the statement that the dreamer presented in his dream? He stresses to himself the need to "do this right." (Remember, we have said that when you recall a question or statement, it's important.)

But let's not get ahead of ourselves; what are some of the unusual details? First of all, such a tall fence suddenly appearing would be a bit unusual, as would the sudden appearance of three huge round-shaped cactuses after you had just been walking through a forest. Now digging up the cactus whole, without leaving any roots, is not all that unusual, but throwing it over that tall fence and not expecting that it would break is a bit out of the ordinary.

Our next job is to determine how objects are working as symbols. What about that fence? Fences generally define territory and include or exclude others. Then there are the cactuses: these can be very prickly, uncomfortable, or even dangerous to handle. It's interesting to note that large cactuses can sometimes take shapes that resemble people with arms. The final symbol is the water, and his reaction to it helps us to verify that the water, indeed, represents an emotional state.

Now that we have all of the elements, let's see what they are telling us. Here's a young man in confusion, wanting to clear things up and to do something correctly. But his problem, as we can see, seems to be territorial. There are "pricklies" in his territory which he needs to remove. He needs to put them on the other side of some sort of barrier or shield, so that he can grow within his own territory. But he must do this without hurting them.

Now two of these "pricklies" can be thrown over the fence—removed from his territory—without being hurt. However, the third one will not take it well. We see a burst of emotion, which strongly affects him, too. So, he has gotten a message that a tough job involving relationships needs to be tackled with care. He will have to be on the look-out, because one of the people involved is going to have an especially hard time leaving his territory. This will cause him great emotional pain, but it needs to be done and "done right" for his own growth to take place—and more than likely for the growth of those he loves to be accomplished, too.

1–4–3

The setting for this dream is a Catholic cathedral; Catholicism is a particular religious denomination, but the word "catholic" also refers to the "church universal." Whichever is being signaled (our feeling is that both senses of the word are important here), the dream has a definite spiritual foundation.

There are only two unusual elements in the dream. First, the statue of Christ behind glass looks at and communicates with the dreamer. Secondly, it communicates with a strange series of hand gestures.

For the dreamer, Christ symbolizes a great spiritual leader, a great teacher, and, at the same time, almost a comfortable friend. Glass is a substance which allows one to see objects or other people but prevents close contact with them. The camera produces a kind of "stop action" which captures and preserves a situation so that one can come back to it later and look at it as often as one likes.

And, though the 1–4–3 signal of the statue was confusing to Pat and Jim as they worked with the dream, it was no problem for the dreamer. She has two young children, and she has established a signal they all use back and forth, when they are in situations where they can't talk to each other but can see each other. One of them holds a hand up and gives the signal she saw in the dream: one finger for "I," four fingers for "love," and three fingers for "you." This is the equivalent of a quick little hug in times of stress.

Suddenly, the whole meaning of the dream was clear. The dreamer was getting the same kind of reassuring "hug" from her higher self, represented by the statue of Christ. Normally, that higher self is closed off from her consciousness (as symbolized by the glass), but even so, it can still find a moment to give her the "I love you" signal—and she can take a picture of it to remind her of this reassurance at some other point when she can use it. Her waking emotion, the sense that "I must be doing something right," was absolutely correct.

The Urinal

The setting here is a bathroom, so we know right away that this dreamer needs to do some cleansing. However, this bathroom is in a public place, not in the dreamer's home. We need to make a note of this. The most unusual detail in this dream is that the wife is physically "equipped" in the same way as her husband.

Now let's look at the symbols we have to work with. First of all, as we have said, there is a public bathroom. This indicates that what is going on in the dream involves something that has been brought out in the open, that has become public knowledge. The only other symbolic aspect of this dream is that his wife has a male organ. He is not the only one with a masculine image. When we see that he is anxious as he wakes up from this dream, we know that he senses a threat to his masculinity. His conscious mind has probably not been able or ready to understand this, but his unconscious feels that he needs to receive this message so that he can cleanse this attitude.

As it happens, when we talked to this young man about his dream, we found that he had recently lost his job, and his wife had taken over the role of supporting the family. This was a situation that was not traditional in his upbringing, and he was being given the awareness that he needed to work at accepting his wife's contribution and not to see it as belittling his own capacities or manhood.

Mother Is an Oyster

There's no real setting here, but we do see a relationship very clearly, so that's what we need to deal with. In fact, the dream begins and ends with communication problems. Unusual details abound here: his mother, after all, is no oyster. And while an oyster's shell often contains sand and debris (that's how it makes pearls, after all), the degree of debris and the fish hook are unusual here.

We really only have a couple of symbols here: the oyster and the fish hook. What does the oyster symbolize? It's a rough creature, with a hard shell that is nearly impossible to pry open, but it's also a creature who has enough patience to produce a pearl. And the fish hook? It's usually barbed, so that it goes in easily and comes out painfully. And if you look at a hook, you see that it turns back towards itself, which can indicate some self-centeredness or selfishness.

So, given all of this, what do we have? Obviously, the mother wants to tell the son something. But because of his perception of her as a hard-shelled, selfish character, living in cold water (right, you caught that—the cold water indicates his feeling that she was emotionally cold), he could not understand whatever it was she was trying to tell him. The message for him was that he needed to be more patient with his mother, so that he could get past the debris and hear what she's trying to tell him. She had a serious need to communicate with him, she was very frustrated about it, and, even though she appeared cold, she really did have something important to tell him—perhaps a pearl of wisdom.

Jesus at Our Party

The setting is the dreamer's home, where he and his wife are hosting a party for their friends. There are only a couple of unusual details: first, that Jesus is a guest at the party, and second, that the plate of food is being handled as if it were communion.

Next let's look at the symbols. There is a table, food, friends, Jesus, and the act of communion. Let's look at each in turn. The table represents service, and in this case, as we look at what's going on in the dream, we can see that the food has a spiritual quality to it. The friends present serve to remind the dreamer of those who surround him each day, helping to make his life what it is.

Jesus, of course, is a most powerful spiritual symbol. His presence in the home and at the party blesses the occasion. It makes this a holy experience.

The final part of the dream, involving the family and the ceremonial presentation of food, serves as a symbol of the communion we all have with each other. A further reinforcement of warmth and love appears in the dream's emphasis that the plate is held "chest-high," connecting it with the dreamer's heart.

Affirmation of life is the spiritual act by which man ceases to live unreflectively.... To affirm life is to deepen, to make more inward, and to exalt the will to live.

Albert Schweitzer

5 | A LIVING DICTIONARY OF DREAM SYMBOLS: TOOLBOX OF THE UNCONSCIOUS

[Man] yet is child, and during all the coming age he must be taught by pictures, symbols, rites, and forms.

The Aquarian Gospel of Jesus the Christ

Reading about dreams can be very helpful. Many good books have been written by people with years of experience in assisting others to understand the messages that come through dreams. The list of references in Chapter 7 contains a number of these books on dreams and related subjects, which we have used and enjoyed.

Several of these books include so-called "dream dictionaries," which list and try to define a large number of objects, qualities, and actions that may appear in our dreams. These dictionaries have been compiled because so many people want to be able to quickly look up, say, "cemetery" or "cat" and find an instant explanation of what that symbol is doing in their dream.

Sometimes this can be helpful. But we do not generally encourage you to use this technique when you are working through your dreams. As we have mentioned, dream symbols have both universal and personal meanings. Most of these dream dictionaries are careful to state that they present only the universal meanings for the dream symbols they include. They clearly explain that the personal meaning of a symbol, what it actually means to a particular dreamer, is not going to be found in their dictionaries; it will only be found as that dreamer searches his or her own mind for the images and feelings and thoughts—the attributes—which arise when the symbol is considered. (If you don't find this clearly stated, be cautious about relying on the meanings that are given in the book.)

You can see that it is a real challenge to create a dream dictionary that would be accurate for each reader. But that is exactly what we've tried to do in the dream dictionary that makes up this chapter. We have created this dream symbol dictionary so that you may enhance the personal meaning you derive from the symbols occuring in your dreams. We have included nearly 350 symbols with their universal meanings, but, alongside most of these, there is space for you to write down the personal meaning of the symbol. In addition, we have provided space throughout the dictionary so that you can add other symbols not already included.

What could be added to the dictionary in the space we have provided? You might jot down some of the feelings you associate with a particular symbol, either before or after it has actually appeared in one of your dreams. You could note the date (or dates) of a particular dream in which the symbol appeared. You might even add a note about a "real-life" experience you have had with the symbol, which may help you understand how it's working in your dreams if it should show up in the future.

Let's look at a specific example to show how this can work. Take the object "motel." A dictionary of dream symbology would explain that "motel" symbolizes a place of temporary residence, which is true in a universal sense. When a dream occurs in a motel setting, it can often be interpreted in a universal sense as being about a transient or temporary situation. Either the situation will soon pass, or the dreamer will move beyond it to some new status; it's just one stop along the road of life. This universal meaning might very well help a dreamer understand the dream more fully.

The motel may not be the setting of the dream, however; it might be simply part of the passing scenery, but it might have a name which is of significance: "Star-Lite Motel," or "Home-Place Inn," or "Daze End Motel," or even "Motel 6." In these cases, if the dreamer focused on transience or impermanence, the true significance of the symbol would be missed. Moreover, if the dreamer, in "real life," works as a desk clerk at a motel or owns and operates a motel, then the symbol's meaning will be nearly the opposite of its universal meaning. For this person, a motel is not a symbol of transience but of permanence.

This is why we offer our "living" dictionary of dream symbols. It will be "all that it can be" only as you begin to add your own meanings to it. And no one can predict the size to which it might grow.

To illustrate how this personalizing of the dream symbol dictionary works, look at one dreamer's sample entries below. On the left are entries which might appear in an "ordinary" dream symbol dictionary; on the right are the meanings which a dreamer might include for each, based on his or her experiences, both in dreams and in "real life." As you can see, when it is presented in this way, the dictionary grows as your dream experience grows, and it soon becomes a very personal document.

Symbolic Meaning	*Personal Meanings*
Clothing: *specifically black clothing: negative attitude, lack of understanding or light.*	*Dreamed on 3/7/90 about wearing a slinky black dress, very sexy; reminded me of that date with Jack back in 1988; exciting, risqué, even a bit risky—but he never called again.*

Symbolic Meaning	Personal Meaning
Neck: *asserting one's will, whether right or wrong; can refer to taking risks, "sticking one's neck out."*	*Takes me back to high school necking sessions. Long swan-like neck is attractive to me; short one is not; Harriet is embarrassed to ever show her neck, always wears scarves.*
	Welding: *Dreamed on 8/10/91 that syrup was being used to weld two pens together so that they became one pen. Joining; sweetness; maybe sweet words (pens are for communicating) to help end a fight with someone.*
Winter: *A time of rest, quiet, hibernation. Coldness, dormancy.*	*Skiing, hockey; dangerous driving conditions; being snowbound on the Merritt Parkway in CT as a child, being wrapped in a blanket and carried through deep snow to spend the night in some stranger's bedroom.*

This dreamer, let's call her Celeste, has used the dictionary in all of the ways described above. In the first entry, she makes a note about a dream which used a symbol (and records the date of the dream, so that in the future she can refer to her dream journal entry for that date to review the dream). When Celeste makes a connection between the slinky dress she was wearing in her dream and a date which the dream brings to mind, the reference to "negative attitude" as a universal meaning for the symbol in the dictionary entry adds a dimension to her understanding. As she works with the dream in her journal, Celeste can use both the universal meaning and her personal meaning to help her interpret the dream's message.

Apparently, Celeste has not yet had a dream which used "neck" as a dream symbol. However, she adds some personal notations to the universal ones listed, which may prove helpful in the future if this symbol does appear in a dream. We see that the word "neck" reminds her of "necking," which is a pun on the word (we'll talk more about the unconscious and puns in a bit) and which was a pretty popular activity for adolescents in this country for many decades but which is not understood as having a universal meaning.

She has also added some other personal material which makes clear how she feels about necks in general. Someday, it may be that Celeste will dream of Harriet and the scarves around her neck; if she reminds herself at that time about what she wrote here, she will then have both the universal meaning, which involves taking risks, and her personal response, which involves Harriet's self-consciousness, to help in understanding how the symbol is used. Since she sees Harriet's actions as being an over-reaction, her unconscious would be able to use the symbol of scarves around Harriet's neck as a short-hand way of saying: "Don't be like Harriet. You don't need to be self-conscious about this (whatever it is); go for it, girl!"

The entry for "Welding" is entirely a personal one. The symbol was not included in the dictionary, but it has appeared in one of Celeste's dreams. She notes the date of the dream, describes how the activity was carried out in her dream, and follows that with the personal meaning she has established for this symbol. She could also, if she wished, make a brief entry under "Pen" and/or "Syrup," so that all three of the elements of this dream are referenced in the dictionary. For these two cross-references, she could either add her personal meaning to the universal one if there is an entry already in the symbol dictionary, or she could write her own under "P" and "S," as appropriate.

"Winter," like "neck," has not yet appeared in Celeste's dreams as a symbol. The universal meaning offered by the symbol entry is offset by Celeste's personal entry. Winter for her seems to be a very active and exciting time, with her emphasis on winter sports and on danger when traveling. When winter appears as the setting in her dreams, it will probably be there to add an element of danger to the actions in the dream.

So, as it presently stands, this symbol dictionary will provide you with universal meanings for many of the symbols that tend to occur in your dreams. But if you feed it, nurture it, help it grow by adding your own ideas, feelings, thoughts, attitudes, and attributes for the symbols already included, you will have a "living" dream symbol dictionary which will prove invaluable as your dream work proceeds.

Before we turn you loose in the dictionary, there are just two more important points to make. One involves the unconscious as a "punster," and the other will show you how symbols can be grouped to better clarify their meanings in dreams.

Word Play in Dreams

Many of us would do well to think of our unconscious as a frustrated stand-up comic. If dreamers fail to take into account the sense of humor within dreams, they may be eliminating many possible interpretations. Jim and Pat are constantly amazed at the original and ingenious plays on words in dreams that function to draw attention to an important point. Here are just a few examples from dreams which have already appeared in this workbook:

- There was the gum-chewing girl in the dream we titled "Chewing Gum" in Chapter 3 who stuck the wad of gum under the table (who "tabled" an issue she was "chewing on").

- Remember the students waiting in line to have their shoes re-soled, again in Chapter 3 (the word play involved "renewing souls")?

- In the dream "Clown Driving Van" from Chapter 4, we see the potential partner as a clown: how often have we heard someone say about someone else, "What a clown!" Here we see the metaphor.

- In that same dream, there is the revealing pun on the name, "Doug Sump"!

- And speaking of names, remember how "Sonja Henie" was used in the dream of the same name? "'S on ya hiney"! Can't beat that for a pun.

These are a few of the puns which you have already seen, but our list could go on and on. In some cases, the dream didn't become clear to us until we stopped pushing and poking at it, relaxed, and let the word-play possibilities have free rein. Here are just a few of the puns and plays on words we have come up with using this type of association:

- A dreamer was chased by Nazis in several dreams; not until we were ready to give up on what the dream might mean did we realize that "Nazis" really meant "Not-Sees." There was something important the dreamer was not seeing.

- In a similar vein, we worked with a dream in which the dreamer was "Russian"—only he wasn't. However, he was a type-A individual, one who was constantly "rushin'" from one task to another. Aha!

- A girl named "Denise" showed up in a dream one night; the dreamer didn't know anyone named Denise. The name appeared so prominently, though, that we knew it was important. It was: the dream was pointing to "da niece" of the dreamer. Aha! again.

- In another dream, a person specifically said, "That's corny; it's a bad joke." Only what he was referring to wasn't corny nor was it a bad joke. We determined that the dream was a physical warning dream, telling the dreamer about a corn allergy which was playing a "bad joke" on his body.

- A Ford car was prominent in a dream; there were constant references to "a Ford"—so many, in fact, that it became clear that the real message of the dream was that the dreamer could not "afford" to make the particular move she was contemplating.

• Actions, too, can be puns: we've worked with several dreams involving diving off high-diving boards into water. The dream is providing a literal representation of a dreamer "diving head-first" into a situation.

Enough! We want you to have the fun of discovering these unique and sometimes uproarious plays on words. And we can promise you they will show up in your dreams. So keep your mind open to puns as you associate attributes and attitudes with your dream symbols.

Symbol Groups

There are a number of symbols that benefit by being grouped with other similar symbols and considered, to some extent, as a whole. This is usually because all of the elements in the group are used in a similar way. For example, colors show up in a dream usually to add information about the emotional state of the dreamer. Different clothes may reflect something about the attitudes and beliefs of the dreamer. Vehicles usually represent the dreamer or some other entity traveling along the path or journey of life. A building often represents the dreamer's physical body; its condition can be an indication of the dreamer's physical well-being.

With this in mind, we have named the appropriate group following an entry when an understanding of the function of the whole group will help to understand how the particular symbol is working. For example,

Bus: (see *Vehicles*): *Someone else is "driving" you; overweight or unusually large; public communication or transportation.*

Turning to "vehicles," you will find a more extensive explanation of how any vehicle, whether it is a bus, a car, a truck, a motorcycle, a skateboard, a subway, a train, a boat, a plane, a blimp, a helicopter, or whatever, is likely to be used as a universal symbol in dreams. Group entries, such as the one for vehicles, are indicated by all capitals, for example: **VEHICLES**.

One exception to this procedure is the entry for "numbers." Because numbers operate in a very unique way, we can only briefly discuss how they may be working in a dream. (Whole books have been written about numerology, the study of numbers as a force in our lives; some of these are listed in Chapter 7 for your further study.) This discussion, as well as a word or two about the universal meaning of each of the numbers from 1 to 12, can be found under the entry for "Numbers," rather than under entries for each of the individual numbers.

You will notice that the dictionary, as it is set up, looks a little bit different from most other dictionaries. In order to allow you to make it your own, we have limited most of our definitions to the left-hand half of each page. This leaves the right-hand side for your notes and personal symbol meanings. The exceptions are the paragraphs on the group names described above. These are generally longer than the other definitions, and they run all the way across the page, so that they will stand out.

The dictionary is also different in that it contains a great deal of blank space. This, too, is to ensure that you, the real creator of the dictionary, have plenty of space for your own notes. It is our hope that, even with the extra space, you will still need to add extra pages to the dictionary in order to record the wealth of symbols that you find in your dream.

We wish you luck—and wonderfully enlightening dreams!

A

Actor or actress: playing a role. _____

Air: one of the four basic elements of life; _____
represents the spiritual, lofty, higher _____
levels of consciousness. _____

Airport: (see *Buildings*) place where _____
ideals, attitude can take flight, move to _____
higher or superconscious level. _____

Alcohol: confusion; lack of control; _____
excess. _____

Amethyst: (see *Gemstones*) translucent _____
purple gemstone; sobriety. _____

ANATOMY: body parts appear in dreams to indicate parts of the body which are experiencing problems or to emphasize parts which need to be put to better use. They frequently work by exaggeration. An very large ear could indicate that the dreamer needs to listen more. Teeth being pushed out of the mouth by the tongue show that the tongue is being used destructively in speech.
A broken foot would indicate a problem with one's spiritual foundations. Unclean hands signify that the dreamer is involved in dirty work of some kind. (See also *Bodily actions*.)

Angel: spiritual guide. _____

ANIMALS: represent a part of the self, often the less spiritual part, and so their presence in dreams helps focus the message. Look at the attitude or emotions usually attached to the animal. Look at its age, the condition of its fur or skin or shell, its behavior. Is it a wild animal, a domestic animal, a mad animal, a caged animal? A cute, cuddly little lion cub is giving one message; a full-grown mature lion on a rampage gives another. Do the animals appear singly in the dream or in herds or flocks or swarms? One small rodent is one small annoyance; hundreds or thousands can be lethal (insects fit this pattern, also).

Apartment: (see *Buildings*) points to a compartment or area of life; not a permanent place, dreamer could move away.

Apple: temptation; in physical dreams, a lack of pectin.

Aqua: (see *Colors*) energy; hard worker.

Aquamarine: (see *Gemstones*) translucent blue-green gemstone; sea water; peaceful, calming, relaxing.

Arena: (see *Buildings*) place of competition, games. Used as dream setting, indicates dreamer's attitude toward life.

Argument: inner questioning or conflict.

Astrological signs: One or more of the astrological signs can appear in dreams to represent the qualities associated with the particular planet or constellation.

Attic: (see *Rooms*) highest level of thinking; superconscious.

B

Baby: new idea, new venture; a new beginning.

Bank: (see *Buildings*) place for storage of valuables; focus on financial matters.

Bar: (see *Buildings*) place of confusion; lack of control.

Barber: one who trims attitudes, shapes and neatens them up.

Barefoot: open to new ideas.

Baseball: (see *Games*)

Basement: (see *Rooms*): unconscious.

Basketball: (see *Games*)

Bathing: (see *Bodily actions*) cleansing; washing away.

Bathroom: (see *Rooms*) place of cleansing, either physical or emotional (as with guilt).

Bear: (see *Animals*) temper.

Bedroom: (see *Rooms*) place of intimacy; sex; rest or sleep.

Bees: (see *Animals*) stinging remarks or actions; a swarm of bees carries a greater sense of danger.

Bicycle: (see *Vehicles*) risky situation, requiring much attention to balance.

Bird: freedom; notice the kind of bird and its color; is the bird nesting or caged up? Is the bird associated with some particular characteristic, as, for example, a parrot or dodo bird?

Birth: some new situation, project, or relationship is coming into the dreamer's life.

Black: (see *Colors*) mystery, unknown; often evil; death. Black and white in sharp contrast indicate a clear distinc-tion between right and wrong.

Blanket: provides warmth, protection; also covers things up.

Blood: kin, close relationship; shedding of blood (esp. of a goat's blood) can indicate sacrifice. Meaning can be destructive or life-giving, depending on how it is used in the dream.

Blue: (see *Colors*) contemplation, reli-gious spirit; high-mindedness; a dark shade of blue can indicate sadness, immersion in work; pale blue shows little depth of character, indicates dreamer is struggling with aspects of maturity.

Boat: (see *Vehicles*) means of traveling along the path of life; note condition, color, whether dreamer or someone else is in charge, dynamics of the water the boat is sailing in, etc.

_____
_____
_____
_____
_____

BODILY ACTIONS: often illustrate dreamer's attitude or opinion about a situation; word plays and puns are frequently involved. Some examples: (a) standing up—dreamer is standing for or taking a stand about something; (b) sitting down—dreamer is sitting down on the job; (c) shaking hands—dreamer is meeting some aspect of self; (d) laughing—humor is needed; (e) fighting—dreamer is at war with self; (f) smoking—angry, hot, disturbed words or actions are involved; (g) eating—some aspect of diet may need examination.

Body parts: (see *Anatomy*)

_____

Bread: money; spiritual food.

_____

Breast: (see *Anatomy*) emphasizes nurturing, mothering aspect of dreamer.

_____
_____
_____

Bride: half of a union; notice what is being joined with the bride. Also denotes that a project is beginning.

_____
_____
_____

Bridge: a symbol of transition, of changing situations. Examine its aspects: is it large? small? high? floating? swinging?

_____
_____
_____
_____

_____
_____
_____
_____
_____

Brother: male aspects, if dreamer is female; similar or contrasting aspects, if dreamer is male. Generally represents person close to dreamer, allowing dream to highlight characteristics of dreamer in unthreatening manner. Can also represent brotherhood of all. (See *Sister*)

Brown: (see *Colors*) earthy; practical attitude; depression.

BUILDINGS: represent facets of dreamer's life (his or her education, job, health, religious status), the state of consciousness or physical state of dreamer. Observe details and condition of building: is it run down? The attitude or body needs repair. Is it rotting? So is the dreamer's attitude. Is it beautiful? The dreamer's consciousness is achieving higher and higher levels of awareness. If the building is the dreamer's residence, what rooms are focused on? What activities are occurring in the residence? If the structure is some building other than the dreamer's residence, what type of activity goes on in that building? In a store, the dreamer is shopping for something. In a repair shop, something of the dreamer's is getting fixed. In a church, the dreamer is seeking spiritual assistance. In an office building, the dreamer is focusing on work. In a sports arena, the dreamer is in competition or is playing games. (Also, see *Rooms*)

Bull: (see *Animals*) hard-headedness; sex.

Burglar: something valuable being stolen from dreamer.

Bus: (see *Vehicles*) Someone else is "driving" you; overweight or unusually large.

C

Camping: temporary residence; moving from one viewpoint to another.

Cancer: uncontrolled growth of the negative; could also represent the zodiac sign, the crab, which is a water creature, thus providing a connection to the emotions.

Castle: (see *Buildings*) lofty, idealistic desires or goals for the self; a romantic notion.

Cathedral: (see *Buildings*) grand, lofty spiritual ideals; high-minded and beautiful values.

Cemetery: place to bury an ideal, a relationship, an object; signifies loss of hope.

Chest area: (see *Anatomy*) love.

Chicken: (see *Animals*) a bird that cannot fly, a cowardly animal. If it's a laying chicken, may be pun on "laying an egg." Note, though, that the egg may be golden!

Christ: spiritual symbol; signifies raising of dreamer's consciousness to the level of the Christ consciousness.

Church: (see *Buildings*) place to seek spiritual assistance, higher level of consciousness.

Circle: (see *Shapes*) indicates unity, completeness.

Citrine: (see *Gemstones*) translucent yellow gemstone; bridges gap between the logical and the intuitive.

Clapping: (see *Bodily actions*) applauding, encouraging an act of the dreamer.

Cleaning: (see *Bodily actions*)

Clock: emphasizes time factor; time shown on face will be significant. For example, 4:15 could mean April 15. (see *Numbers*)

Closet: place to store unused items or things from the past.

CLOTHING: The clothing worn in a dream represents the attitudes "worn" by the dreamer. Consider the colors of the clothes, the condition, whether or not they are appropriate or inappropriate for the activity and season of the dream. Do the clothes fit the wearer? Do they represent a profession or job? Old tattered clothes can represent outgrown attitudes; on the other hand, brand-new clothes or clothes which still have price tags attached could indicate ideas the dreamer is only just beginning to be familiar with. A lack of clothing, nakedness, can point to an openness to criticism, vulnerability. A hat highlights the activities of mind; at the same time, it covers the hair, which represents the dreamer's thought processes or way of thinking. Shoes represent the dreamer's spiritual foundation; overshoes add an element of protection to that symbol.

Coat: (see *Clothing*) attitude or emotion covering the dreamer; a red coat (see *Colors*) can indicate anger or a bad attitude.

_____
_____
_____
_____

Cold: aloof.

_____

College: (see *Buildings*) high level of learning.

_____
_____

COLORS: usually provide some indication of dreamer's emotions or mental condition. Observe characteristics of the colors: bright vivid colors often convey positive atmosphere; pale colors can indicate an immature level of the particular emotion; muddy colors can indicate negative tendencies; washed-out colors represent a weariness or worn-down attitude. See individual colors.

Convenience store: (see *Buildings*) emphasizes doing something quickly, but higher price is paid.

_____
_____
_____

Courtroom: (see *Rooms*) indicates need for justice, for making a fair decision; potential pun on "courting"—who's courting the dreamer?

_____
_____
_____
_____

Cow: (see *Animals*) laziness; contemplation; fertility; nurturing.

_____
_____

Crossroad: point of decision; dreamer needs to decide which way to go.

_____
_____

_____
_____
_____
_____
_____
_____

Crawling: (see *Bodily actions*) slow movement toward something; if crawler is a baby, this is normal as dreamer develops abilities in particular arena of life; if more mature person is crawling, some difficulty is present.

Craziness: no use of reason in a given situation (See *Idiocy*.)

Cross: (see *Shapes*) Christian symbol; symbol of sacrifice; symbol of Red Cross, indicating assistance, help, support.

Crowing: boasting or gloating.

Crown: represents an award for an attitude; royalty.

Cultures: If other than dreamer's own culture, denotes foreignness; look at beliefs held about the culture, stereotypical features of the culture.

Curtains: closed, these symbolize a blockage of light or understanding.

D

Dance: following the rhythm of life; two people dancing well together indicate a harmonious relationship. May also indicate following a partner's lead.

Death: change of consciousness; some aspect of dreamer's life—relationship, attitude, job—is over or leaving. Rarely refers to death of dreamer.

Desert: arid, barren land; lack of spiritual element (see *Water*); loneliness.

Diamond: (see *Gemstones*) clear, colorless gemstone; greed, hardness; marriage symbol; exposes the ego.

Dining room: (see *Rooms*) food, both physical or spiritual; banquet of ideas or beliefs.

Dinosaur: (see *Animals*) an old or outdated way of doing things.

Doctor: healer; may point to a physical need for something.

Dog: (see *Animals*) faithfulness or unfaithfulness; indiscriminate sex; a pack of barking dogs can mean that a group of people is talking about dreamer; may represent a warning.

Door: entrance to or exit from some part of your life or some opportunity; is it locked or unlocked? Do you have the key? Opening front door can indicate a receptiveness to new (especially spiritual) ideas. Door can also point to a physical closing or blockage: closing or locking a back door, for example, can indicate blocking the body's means of elimination; constipation.

Dress shop: (see *Buildings*) place to shop for new attitudes.

Drowning: (see *Bodily actions*) a very emotional situation, where dreamer can't get enough of the air/spiritual qualities needed for survival; can also indicate a physical condition involving the lungs.

Drunkenness: confusion, lack of control; deviation from what is accepted.

Dry cleaner's: (see *Buildings*) place to take attitudes or beliefs for cleansing, purifying.

Dying: (see *Bodily actions* and *Death*) ending of old situation or attitude.

E

Ears: (see *Anatomy*) emphasizes dreamer's ability—or lack of ability—to hear the truths of his or her life.

Earth: one of the four basic elements of life; emphasizes the practical, down-to-earth side of the dreamer; if exaggerated presence, can represent dreamer's tendency to grovel.

Eating: (see *Bodily actions*) some aspect of diet may need examination; something is "eating away" at dreamer.

Egg: new idea or project, nearly ready to hatch; renewal of life.

Elevator: significant change of consciousness; is it going up or down? Can be sexual.

Emerald: (see *Gemstones*) translucent green gemstone; healing, curative powers; antidote to sickness.

Enemy: aspect of dreamer involved in internal conflict.

Escalator: moderate change of consciousness.

Evening: available light is failing, as is dreamer's understanding of subject. Something or some relationship is drawing to a close.

Explosion: turmoil, extreme confusion; letting repressed emotions loose.

_____
_____

Eyes: (see *Anatomy*) represent dreamer's vision, inner way of seeing things; a single eye would represent the third eye, which stands for the dreamer's intuition, precognition. Note whether glasses are worn, and what conditions the glasses are in. (See *Glasses*.)

_____
_____
_____
_____
_____
_____

F

Fall: time to harvest, prepare for cold.

_____

Falling: (see *Bodily actions*) failing, "falling down on the job."

_____
_____

Father: authority figure; male quality; for women, the animus; can symbolize God.

_____
_____
_____

Fence: a barrier to enclose, to protect, or to restrict the entry of others. Can sometimes be used to set apart and delineate a field of endeavor.

_____
_____
_____
_____

Fighting: (see *Bodily actions*) dreamer is at war, usually with self.

_____
_____

Fire: one of the four basic elements of life; depending on how it's used, it can represent a cleansing force, a destructive force, or a raging temper.

_____
_____
_____

FIREARMS: shooting a rifle, gun, or other weapon can indicate either sexual activity or an argument with self; also possible word play on "shooting off at the mouth." Note who is holding the firearm: a gun in a child's hands would indicate indiscriminate, immature sexual activity.

Fireplace: anger or warmth and coziness, depending on the associated aspects; in physical dreams, points to fevered or ailing part of the body.

_____
_____
_____
_____

Fish: (see *Animals*) symbol of Christianity; spiritual food. A school of fish could carry connotations of a learning situation.

_____
_____
_____
_____

Fishing: (see *Bodily actions*) seeking new spiritual attitudes or path.

_____
_____

Fleas, flies: (see *Animals*) small annoyances or irritations.

_____
_____

Flood: (see *Water*) surge of overwhelming, destructive emotion.

_____
_____

Floor: foundation of attitudes, beliefs. Note the condition of the floor: if it is sinking, the foundation is not a reliable one; if floor is rough and even, so are the beliefs.

_____
_____
_____
_____

FLOWER: holds various symbolic meanings. Note whether the flower is a hothouse variety, a wildflower, or a weed; note its color, whether it serves as a state flower. Note the characteristics given to particular flowers, the romantic uses of the rose, the highly religious symbolism of the lily, the simple country flavor of the daisy. Note any connections of the flower with a holiday, song, literature, or poetry.

Flying: freedom, lack of restriction; movement into higher consciousness or sphere.

Football: (see *Games*)

Forest: represents a blockage of vision of what's ahead. Examine aspects, response to it: Is it a wild, fearful place? Is it a beautiful, calm soothing place?

Fork: decision point along life's path.

Fort: (see *Buildings*) indicates dreamer's need to defend from attacks by others, or by current situation.

Freeway: path of life, with emphasis on faster road, easy way; ask "Who is paying my way on this path?"

Frog: (see *Animals*) tendency to jump around; aspects include large mouth, warts.

Funeral: end of old situation; a closing off or burying of an enterprise, a relationship, or an aspect of the dreamer's life.

Furniture: especially in a house, indicates dreamer's attitudes, the beliefs with which he or she furnishes his life; notice style, condition, other aspects.

G

GAMES: Dreams offer guidance about life, a serious subject. When games appear, they often indicate that something is being treated as play. Look at the aspects: is it a child's game? who are the players? what are the emotions? Games also introduce competition. Two or more attitudes are vying for the dreamer's attention or acceptance. Note which one is winning, what it represents.

Garage: (see *Buildings*) place to store unused items from past; place to repair the body.

Gas station: (see *Buildings*) place to find energy, fuel; if female dreamer, can represent sex.

Gate: opening, beginning; start of something new.

GEMSTONES: gemstones and jewels have long been considered to convey special powers to their wearers. For example, the amethyst, universally held to represent sobriety, is sometimes called the "Bishop's stone," and bishops in the Catholic church still wear the stone to symbolize their moral victory over worldly pleasures. More can be understood about gemstones, too, by looking at their colors.

Ghost: represents an aspect of the past (usually spiritual).

Giraffe: (see *Animals*) willfulness; sticking one's neck out.

Giving birth: (see *Bodily actions*) beginning a new project, idea, attitude.

Glasses: (see *Anatomy*) used to magnify or clarify vision of dreamer.

Gloves: (see *Clothing*) indicate something requires careful handling; could indicate a covering up of the hands, the tools of service; could also indicate an unwillingness to get hands dirty.

Gnats: (see *Animals*) small irritations and annoyances.

God: highest spiritual authority; Creator.

Gold: precious object, ideal, enlightened attitude.

Gorilla: (see *Animals*) emphasis on the physical at the expense of the mental.

Grass: cushion or grounding; healing (see *Green*); marijuana.

Grave: place of burial of attitudes, relationships, and so on; time is up for something.

Gray: (see *Colors*) confusion; inability to choose.

Green: (see *Colors*) shows healing, strength; bluish-green or muted green colors point to jealousy or untrustworthiness.

Grocery store: (see *Buildings*) concerned with nutrition, food, diet.

Gum: an issue the dreamer is "chewing" on; something sticky.

Gun: (see *Firearms*)

H

Hair: thought processes of the dreamer; notice condition and texture.

Hall or **hallway**: (see *Rooms*) transition state between two situations.

Hammer: a driving force; possible pun on "hammering" home a point.

Hands: (see *Anatomy*) signify service; beautiful hands would indicate exemplary service, while unclean hands, with broken, jagged nails would indicate the opposite.

Heart: represents instinctual mode rather than intellectual, as in "follow your heart"; love; can point to physical problem. A breaking heart could represent emotional pain.

Highway: the path of life, life's journey stretching ahead of the dreamer. Note the condition of the road surface, the type of country it is running through, the number of lanes it has, whether it is straight or windy.

Hill: an obstacle on the path of life; spiritual ascent (see *Mountain*).

Hog: (see *Animals*) taking more than one's share; dominating.

Home: (see *Buildings*) as with "house," represents dreamer's body; condition of home indicates condition of dreamer's body.

Honey: sweetness, stickiness.

Horse: (see *Animals*) freedom; sexual power.

Hospital: (see *Buildings*) place of healing; focus on health.

Hotel: (see *Buildings*) temporary state of consciousness or temporary situation.

House: (see *Buildings*) as with "home," represents dreamer's body; consider aspects of house to determine condition of body.

House trailer: temporary situation or physical condition in dreamer's life.

Hurricane: a huge emotional storm, involving lots of anger and destruction; very frightening situation.

I

Ice: lack of feeling, emotional coldness; if ice is thin, it signals a dangerous situation. (See *Water*.)

Idiocy: stupidity, lack of reason in dealing with situation (see *Craziness*).

Indigo: (see *Colors*) religious quest.

Insect: something which may be "bugging" the dreamer. Note kind and quantity of insects. (See *Animals*.)

Intercourse (sexual): intimate interpersonal communication.

J

Jade: (see *Gemstones*) opaque green gemstone; link between the spiritual and the mundane.

Jellyfish: weakness, ineffectiveness in dreamer; signals need to make decisions, take charge of life.

Jesus: spiritual teacher.

Jewelry store: (see *Buildings*) place to shop for valuable, priceless qualities with which to adorn inner self.

Jewels: (see *Gemstones*) treasures of the mind and value system; ideals; morals.

K

Key: tool to use to open doors, get inside oneself or a situation, solve a problem. Note appearance of key, consider what it unlocks in the dream.

Kiss: close communication, intimacy; notice aspects, such as length, kind of kiss.

Kitchen: (see *Rooms*) service, preparation; nutrition or dietary need.

Knife: cutting words; sex.

L

Ladder: way to climb to a higher level, a better situation, than presently exists for dreamer or to fall to a lower level; can also symbolize a connection between the consciousness and the unconsciousness.

Lake: (see *Water*) reservoir of emotion.

Lamb: (see *Animals*) gentle defenseless creature; represents Christ; used as sacrifice.

Lapis lazuli: (see *Gemstones*) opaque blue; self-assurance; considered to have mystical qualities.

Laughing: (see *Bodily actions*) more humor needed in situation; dreamer taking self too seriously.

Left: choosing a left-hand object is choosing from the dreamer's past; a choice from the left is often a liberal choice, a wrong choice, or a choice made out of habit.

Left to right motion: motion from left to right indicates going into the future, going in the right direction; can mean movement toward masculine tendencies.

Letter: means of communication; if words can be read, they are significant.

Light switch: control of understanding; are you turning a light on or off a given situation?

Living room: (see *Rooms*) place where the family lives, communicates, and carries out daily activities; focus is on the family as a whole.

Loss, losing: (see *Bodily actions*) generally refers to spiritual values; loss of a valuable can indicate physical problem.

M

Mailbox: communication (note addresses, postmarks on letters, if visible); boxed in.

Mall: seeking for new attitudes in sheltered area; large number of options.

Maroon: (see *Colors*) poor health; possible pun on being "marooned on a desert isle."

Marriage: a merging or joining with another or with a higher aspect of oneself; note the type of ceremony, other aspects.

Medicine: something the dreamer must do or take, usually not too pleasant, in order to return to health, to right-mindedness; note pun on "a bitter pill to swallow."

Microscope: provides dreamer with a close look at something, great magnification of a situation; enlarges something out of normal proportion. (See *Telescope*)

Milk: represents nourishment, mothering; note pun on "milk of human kindness"; can be used to signal a physical problem, perhaps an allergy.

Monster: fearful situation confronting or chasing dreamer; can represent an "awful" truth dreamer is trying to run away from.

_____
_____
_____
_____

Motel: (see _Buildings_) situation is temporary.

_____
_____

Motion: shows dreamer's attitude: (a) slow motion indicates being bogged down in something; (b) speeded-up motion shows a rushing into something; (c) lack of motion indicates frozen attitude, being completely incapacitated in some way; (d) motion away from something indicates avoidance, flight, fear. (See _Left_ and _Right_.)

_____
_____
_____
_____
_____
_____
_____
_____

Mountain: a path which travels up a mountain usually provides dreamer a very high, spiritual overview of his or her life (See _Hill._)

_____
_____
_____
_____

Mouth: (see _Anatomy_) origination of speech, words.

_____
_____

Movie: presents a story of the dreamer's self.

_____
_____

Music: harmony; the rhythm with which life moves for the dreamer. Examine the tempo, and the type of music. Pay close attention to the title and words of a song, if they are part of the dream.

_____
_____
_____
_____
_____

_____
_____

N

Nakedness: extreme vulnerability; openness, exposure of self.

Neck: (see *Anatomy*) "sticking his or her neck out," taking risks; asserting one's will, whether right or wrong.

Neighbor: usually represents some aspect of the dreamer (use the technique of asking for two or three attributes to discover which aspect).

Nest: secure, cozy home.

NUMBERS: have long held special emotional and magical qualities. Edgar Cayce notes they represent strength or weakness, assets or deterrents, change or stability. Birthdates, anniversaries should be looked at for their emotional resonances. Other numbers appearing in dreams should be summed: Add the numbers together; the resulting digit is significant. For example, 555-3671 = 5+5+5+3+ 6+7+1 = 32 = 3 + 2 = 5. Following Cayce's interpretations, the numbers from 1 to 12 signify:

1 = unity; source; basis for all other numbers, great strength

2 = duality (even numbers are weaker than odd numbers)

3 = trinity, great strength (1 + 2, 2 + 1, or 2 against 1)

4 = body; 4 corners of earth; 40 (higher 4) = cleansing, testing

5 = activity; immediate change

6 = beauty, symmetrical force, strength (two 3s)

7 = spiritual forces, mystical relationship, or completion

8 = vacillation (double the weakness or strength of 4)

9 = completion; termination of natural order; a finish

10 = completion of extraordinary strength; return to the 1

11 = presents both beauty and weakness

12 = replenishing of spiritual strength; end and beginning

O

Ocean: huge emotional vastness; note its state, its color.

Office: place where work takes place on a situation; dreamer in an office setting is working on something.

Office building: (see *Buildings*) site of work, business activities; note the level of the building on which dream action occurs.

Old person: can represent wisdom and experience; gray hair emphasizes this.

Onyx: (see *Gemstones*) opaque black gemstone; drives away bad temper; prevents loss of energy.

Opal: (see *Gemstones*) milky white gemstone; symbolizes love; restores vision and memory.

Orange: (see *Colors*) thoughtfulness; sexual energy. A golden orange indicates vitality and self-control; a brownish orange shows laziness, a lack of ambition.

P

Paralysis: state of inaction, inability to move in a situation; usually the result of fear.

Party: social gathering; note guests, the food and drink served, the general atmosphere.

Peacock: emphasis on false front, pride, vanity, need for self-gratification.

Pearl: (see *Gemstones*) round white gemstone; patience; transformation; purity.

Pen or **pencil**: means of direct communication. Note size of instrument, any words written.

Penthouse: (see *Rooms*) a wealth of superconscious ideas; probably not a permanent state.

Photograph: action has been stopped so that dreamer can see more clearly.

Pink: (see *Colors*) immaturity in love; happiness.

Pistol: (see *Firearms*)

Play: (see *Games*)

Policeman: higher authority; need to police a situation, use self-control.

Pond (see *Water*): emotional situation, not as overwhelming as is represented by a lake or an ocean.

_____
_____
_____

Pregnancy: birth of new idea or project; note stage of pregnancy, mother's condition, emotional state.

_____
_____
_____

Prison: (see *Buildings*) indicates dreamer's sense of being trapped, constricted, restrained by present life situation or by dreamer's self-imposed rules and restrictions.

_____
_____
_____
_____

Purple: (see *Colors*) regal, royal; strong shade can show tendency to be overbearing.

_____
_____
_____

2

Quartz: (see *Gemstones*) clear gemstone; amplification.

_____
_____

Queen: high authority, feminine principles; can point to lofty, self-important attitude.

_____
_____
_____

Quicksand: lack of solid foundation for beliefs, attitudes, ideals; foundation falling away under dreamer, lack of stability.

_____
_____
_____
_____

R

Race: points to fast movement along journey of life, with added element of competition against self or against the clock; rivalry.

Radio: direct communication to dreamer. Note message radio is sending, music playing on the station, etc.

Rain: washing away of life's dirt and grime; emotional cleansing; anxiety.

Rainbow: a signal of hope, upcoming spiritual renewal.

Rape: violation of dreamer's self, principles, ideals; a forcing of some issue before its time.

Red: (see *Colors*) force, vigor, energy; anger; sexual energy; indicates to stop doing something. A dark red, either vivid or understated, points to inner turmoil, frustration.

Repair shop: place where dreamer's attitudes, relationships, physical condition could be changed, improved, otherwise fixed.

Restaurant: (see *Buildings*) place where dreamer is served food (for thought, for spiritual nourishment); can point to physical problems relating to diet.

Rifle: (see *Firearms*)

Right: the choice of the right-hand
object symbolizes the right choice, the
conservative choice, or a new way of
doing things.

Right to left motion: movement from
right to left indicates movement into
the past, toward a wrong decision; can
mean movement toward feminine
tendencies.

Road: path or journey in life.

Rocks: obstacles, unpleasantness in the
journey ahead; attitude problem—as
with hard-headedness, or "rocks in the
head." Possible pun on "on the rocks."

ROOMS: as with buildings, rooms represent various attitudes, states of consciousness, or physical states of dreamer. The condition of the rooms, how they are
decorated, items that are missing or out of place in the room should all be carefully observed. Is the room the attic or basement? What floor of the building is
the room on? Upper stories would point to activities of the higher consciousness;
lower stories would be reserved for activities of lower levels of consciousness.
Note the type of activity which normally takes place in the room: this will aid in
understanding how it is being used in relation to the dreamer. (See *Buildings*.)

Rose: (see *Flowers*)

Rose-pink: (see *Colors*) love, joy.

Ruby: (see *Gemstones*) clear red
gemstone; vitality; stone of courage;
cleanses the blood.

S

Sailboat: (see *Vehicles*) a means of traveling along life's path; note the condition of the boat, the color of the sails, the dynamics and color of the water the boat sails in.

Sapphire: (see *Gemstones*) clear blue gemstone; calming, relaxing; promotes clear thinking.

Scarlet: (see *Colors*) overdose of ego, passion.

School: (see *Buildings*) place of learning; level of school indicates level of learning; that is, elementary school is lower level; high school is upper level, and so on.

Scissors, shears: can indicate cutting short a life or the life of some attitude or belief; can also indicate the "cutting" effects of words or actions.

Sex: (see *Intercourse*)

Shaking hands: (see *Bodily actions*) dreamer is meeting some aspect of self.

SHAPES: Shapes can have very important meanings in dreams, as in life. For example, people sitting at a round table can be thought of as working in unison, whereas those same people at a square table may be seen as experiencing antagonism—each person taking a side in the discussion. Two lines crossing each other might represent the Christian cross or an "X" which marks a spot.

Ship: (see *Vehicles*) means of traveling along the journey of life; control not usually in the dreamer's hands; can signal obesity.

Shoe store: (see *Buildings*) place to shop for new foundations, beliefs.

Shopping: (see *Bodily actions*) searching for new attitudes, beliefs; signals a need to make choices, to pay for what is sought after.

Shopping center: (see *Buildings*) place to search for new attitudes.

Showering: (see *Bodily actions*) cleansing; washing away.

Sister: female aspects of self, if dreamer is male; similar or contrasting aspects, if dreamer is female. Generally represents person close to dreamer, allowing dream to highlight characteristics of dreamer in unthreatening manner. Can also represent sisterhood of all. (See *Brother*.)

Sitting: (see *Bodily actions*) dreamer is "sitting down on the job" or "sitting on an idea."

Skating: (see *Bodily actions*) in a danger- ous situation ("skating on thin ice") or possibly out of control.

Skipping: (see *Bodily actions*) possible pun: skipping something the dreamer needs to see.

Sky: a higher level; the limits.

Snake: (see *Animals*) temptation, sex; wisdom.

Solar plexus: (see *Anatomy*) emotions.

Soldier: military authority figure; empha- sis on discipline; battle. Observe cond- itions of battle, what is being fought over, size of opposing armies, color of uniform.

Spring: new birth; time of beginning.

Square: (see *Shapes*) shows opposition, karmic forces at work.

Stairs, stairway: climbing to another level of consciousness or awareness. If movement is down the stairs, sig- nals a loss of confidence. Note where stairs begin and end, how steep they are, whether they are straight, curved, or angled.

Standing: (see *Bodily actions*) dreamer is standing for or taking a stand on something.

Star: (see *Shapes*) can signal change; an award or prize; ancient belief held that the five points represent the four elements (earth, water, fire, and air) dominated by the mind.

Stomach: (see *Anatomy*) probably indicating an inability to digest or assimilate something, either emotionally or physically.

Store: (see *Buildings*) place to shop for new things: attitudes, jobs, relationships, other situations.

Stump: life is gone from something; dead roots; disfigurement.

Summer: growing time; time to cultivate; good times; heat.

Sword: instrument which can cut, like knife, but inflicts deeper more dangerous wounds; can represent words and actions which can be truly lethal. Note its condition, who wields it.

T

Table: work place, place where people are served, place of service; in kitchen, table can hold objects relating to physical condition, diet. Note color, condition of table, objects on it, activities occurring at or around it.

Teacher: aspect of self which can provide learning.

Teeth: (see *Anatomy*) used in speech; biting words or actions.

Telephone: direct communication with another or with self; note carefully what is said.

Telescope: provides dreamer with a look far into the distance; brings what is distant up close. (See *Microscope*.)

Television: generally presents dreamer with his or her own story, situation. Can also present a direct message or communication.

Toilet: place to rid body or self of unnecessary, unwanted attitudes or attributes.

Topaz: (see *Gemstones*) smoky yellow gemstone; stone of strength; especially for women, works to cure ailments specific to women.

Tower: (see *Rooms*) superconscious mind, highest level of consciousness. This also applies to a room located on the highest level of a building.

Toy store: (see *Buildings*) place to shop for childlike or childish attitudes.

Tractor, or other heavy equipment: deals with cultivation of a big project or work effort.

Traffic signs: give directions which can be applied to dreamer's situation: stop, yield, turn, one way, and so on.

Train: (see *Vehicles*) means of moving along one's path in life; somewhat restricted by direction in which tracks are laid; powerful, nearly unstoppable force.

Trap: pitfall in life; error or poor attitude which constrains or restricts or imprisons the dreamer.

Tree: provider of nourishment, shelter; strong, tall; can also point to dreamer's roots, interconnectedness of family.

Triangle: (see *Shapes*) the godhead, trinity; can have spiritual meaning; may indicate problems of a three-way relationship.

Truck: this is a work vehicle; the dream is dealing with a job or work situation.

Tunnel: connection between this life and the next; transition without natural light.

Turquoise: (see *Gemstones*) opaque blue-green gemstone; balancing and healing energy; unifying force between earth-bound and spiritual elements.

U

University: (see *Buildings*) place of higher learning.

Urine: substance which carries waste and toxins from body; represents cleansing process. Usually indicates dream is concerned with a physical problem.

Uterus: motherhood; place where new ideas are nurtured and developed.

V

VEHICLES: represent the dreamer's movement along life's path. Is the vehicle moving quickly or slowly? Is the vehicle in good condition? What kind of vehicle is it? Blimps, buses, ships, and other large vehicles often signal over-weight, both physical and emotional. Skateboards, scooters, motorcycles, and bicycles indicate extra attention to balance, either emotionally or physically. Notice who is controlling or driving the vehicle; who is behind the wheel (if the vehicle has a wheel). Note also condition, color, size, make, model, and any extra or unusual accessories. Pay attention to the road or track or waterway the vehicle is traveling upon, the scenery, the passengers, and whether the vehicle has enough fuel. If the vehicle is a car, it often represents the dreamer's physical body: in such cases, note the condition of the vehicle and any damage or mal-functioning. For example, headlights represent eyes; fenders represent hips; wheels/tires represent legs and/or feet; heating/cooling system represents circulatory system; motor represents various internal organs; and pedals and steering wheel represent the dreamer's means of controlling his or her body.

Violet: (see *Colors*) represents search for spiritual truth. _____

W

Wall: obstacle in dreamer's path; can indicate that dreamer is blocking acceptance of a new idea. Can point to blockage in physical body. _____

Wallet: place for storing personal valuables, ideals, morals, beliefs. _____

Warehouse: (see *Buildings*) storehouse of material dreamer could use for creative activities.

Water: one of the four basic elements of life, symbolizing spiritual and emotional aspects. Note the dynamics of the water: is it a smooth, deep-flowing river or a raging set of rapids and waterfalls? Is it a mirror-smooth lake or a wildly tossing ocean? Is there ice on the water? Is there a complete lack of water, as in a desert? Is water being drawn from a well? This would show the dreamer receiving "water of life," spiritual guidance.

Wheel: symbolizes unity, unending movement, completion; if seen as the wheel of a car, can be referring to dreamer's foot or leg, may be pointing to a physical problem. Note use of wheel to indicate going round and round over something or even "spinning one's wheels."

White: (see *Colors*) purity; positive attitude. Black and white in sharp contrast indicate a clear distinction between right and wrong.

Window: an opening into or out of a structure; is it open or shut?

Winter: a time of cold, dormancy, of rest, quiet, hibernation.

_____

_____

Work room: (see *Rooms*) place to repair, maintain, or build new attitudes and beliefs.

_____

_____

_____

X

....

X: (see *Shapes*) can mark a spot, indicate a crossroads in dreamer's life.

_____

_____

X-ray: examination of dreamer's inner self.

_____

_____

Y

....

Y: (see *Shapes*) shows a fork, a point of choice, in dreamer's life path.

_____

_____

Yellow: (see *Colors*) mental activity; fear and cowardice.

_____

_____

_____

_____

_____

_____

_____

_____

Z

Z: A final element, last in line.

Zebra: (see *Animals*) as with horse, possible sexual meaning; also points to mixture of positive (white) and negative (black).

Zoo: place where dreamer's lower levels of consciousness can be displayed in their (nearly) natural state. (See *Animals*.)

_____

_____

_____

_____

_____

_____

_____

_____

_____

_____

_____

_____

_____

_____

_____

_____

_____

_____

_____

6 | A Little Out of the Ordinary: Dessert for Dreamers

There is a dreamer dreaming us....

African Bushman

We have saved some material that we felt would be too distracting in the earlier chapters. Here we will briefly touch on past-life dreams, lucid dreams, and dreaming for others. But first, let us begin with one of our favorite exercises. This is a "waking mind trip," in which you are led through a waking dream and then shown how this experience can give you some insight into where you are in your life.

A "Waking Mind Trip"

A number of years ago, Pat and Jim attended a seminar on dreams sponsored by the Association for Research and Enlightenment (ARE), an organization founded on the principles set forth by Edgar Cayce, the so-called "Sleeping Prophet." The seminar was led by Judith Sherbenou and included an exercise in which participants, with eyes closed, were led on a "trip" in their minds. When the trip was over, the experience was analyzed as if it were a dream. In this way, the participants were given a vivid example of how dreams work and how they may be understood.

After the seminar, Judy graciously gave Jim and Pat permission to use the seminar in their own work. Now, when Jim and Pat conduct their dream seminars every month or two in the south Texas area, a "waking mind trip" is almost always included. Students are told to suspend their use of logic and reasoning, make themselves comfortable, close their eyes, and follow Pat as she leads them on an imaginary walk. Her promise is that, if they follow her guidance, they will experience a number of revelations about their lives: where they are on their journey, what problems they are dealing with, and what resources they have for dealing with those problems.

Of course, this is a book and not a face-to-face encounter with Pat and Jim, so we suggest that you find someone to read the instructions out loud while you mentally follow them. This person could be your dream partner, though we suggest a third person so that both you and your dream partner can participate in the experience without any pre-knowledge of where you will be going on the dream walk.

Then, when the walk is over, you will need to be ready to answer some questions. We've provided a page with questions and room for your answers. Look ahead and find that page; feel free to make copies of it for yourself and any others who may be taking the walk along with you.

The material to be read aloud is presented in italics on the next two pages. We suggest that this material be read slowly, allowing time for those on the trip to mentally answer the questions asked along the way. The whole trip should take about five to seven minutes. When the questions have been answered, return to the pages following the reading, and we will show you how to make sense of the things that happened to you on the trip.

Sit in a comfortable position, either on the floor or on a chair. Be sure that neither clothing nor shoes are constricting you in any way. Perhaps the lighting could be dimmed somewhat, though the room should not be dark. When everyone is ready, the reader should begin reading from the top of the next page.

Enjoy your trip!

❊ *Close your eyes and try to empty your mind of any concerns or anxieties for the next few minutes. Observe your breath as it flows in and out; tune in to the rhythm of your body. Visualize breathing in calmness, breathing out stress.*

❊ *Relax your toes, your feet, your leg muscles, your torso, your fingertips, your arms, your shoulders, your neck, your jaw, your facial muscles, your forehead. Notice that you're deeply relaxed. Imagine yourself getting into your own bed, getting comfortable, and beginning to drift off. You're entering another realm, the realm of dreams.*

❊ *Your dream opens with you standing in a field. Is it day or night?*

❊ *What season of the year is it?*

❊ *Look down at your feet and notice their appearance.*

❊ *There's a forest in the distance, and you begin to move toward it. You can smell the air and feel it on your face, and you know exactly the color of the sky. All of your senses are alert. You can hear the sounds of insects and small animals. You are very, very aware.*

❊ *You enter the forest now, and there's a path which you take. As you walk down the path, you notice that the colors and the smells are changing.*

❊ *Up ahead, you see a fork in the path. At the fork, you must make a decision. Which way will you go? You decide, and continue in that direction.*

❧ You hear a sound behind you, but you're not startled; everything's fine, and you continue on the path.

❧ It's getting darker, and the sounds are getting louder, and again you hear a sound behind you. You become very aware that something or someone is following you. You're feeling some anxiety; you're moving faster and trying to outdistance whatever is there.

❧ In your haste to escape whatever it is, you stumble and fall. But you have a weapon at your disposal, and with it, you subdue and repel whatever has been following you.

❧ At this point, you stop and ask the creature a question: "Why are you chasing me?" You listen very carefully for the answer.

❧ Now that you have your answer, you demand that the creature give you a gift. You don't ask for this gift, you demand it. Pay very close attention to the gift that you are given.

❧ This is the end of the dream. Focus on your breathing once again, notice your body rhythm and the flow of your breath. When you are once again in full possession of your consciousness, open your eyes.

❧ This is the end of the reading. Now write down all of the specific decisions you made in your dream, using the list of questions provided. When every question is answered, we'll return to the book for help in understanding the experience.

In the waking mind trip:

What is the season? _____

_____

Is it day or night? _____

_____

What is on your feet? _____

_____

Which fork of the path do you choose? _____

_____

Which of your senses predominates? _____

_____

How do you react to the forest? _____

_____

What is chasing you? _____

_____

Why is it following you? _____

_____

What is your weapon? _____

_____

What is the gift that is given to you? _____

_____

At what point do you feel fear? _____

_____

To what extent are you fearful? _____

_____

About the Waking Mind Trip

This exercise serves in a way as a generic dream: it contains common dream symbols, and it requires you to make decisions, just as in your own dreams. It puts you in a situation with an uncertain outcome, and you can watch yourself as you handle things. By looking at the reactions and decisions you make in this generic dream, you can gain information about what's going on in your life right now. Look at each of the answers you gave as we discuss the meaning of each question.

What is the season? Your choice can tell you about the general atmosphere in your life at this time or what cycle you are in. Winter is a dormant, hibernating time, possibly including some depression. People actively involved in following a goal rarely choose winter. Spring represents new growth, beginnings, seeds planted, life. Summer is the time when your awareness about what you want to do and where you want to go is in full bloom; it is a time for cultivating. Fall evokes the harvest, and the ability to reap the benefits of earlier efforts.

Of course, there are the literal-minded who say, "Well, it's fall today, so of course it's fall in my dream." But even this response indicates that you are not feeling strongly drawn to the other seasons and their associations, which can be important information.

Is it day or night? Most people choose daytime; they want to operate in situations where light is available both to see by and to understand by. Is it morning, when things are fresh and the day is just beginning? Perhaps it is high noon, with work in full progress and lots of light and warmth? Or is it late afternoon or early evening, when things are winding down, the light is softer, less glaring, and a rest period is ahead.

Note that, if you have chosen nighttime, it can be a sign that you are really not ready to receive knowledge about your situation.

What is on your feet? Bare feet could signal a receptivity and openness to the unknown. Are you wearing dress shoes? Army boots? Hiking shoes? Sandals? Each of these choices gives an indication of your attitude and what you anticipate lies ahead of you.

Which fork in the path do you choose? When you reached the fork you had to make a decision. If you took a left path—and you chose fall for the season at the start of the walk—this may be a sign that you're doing things for left-brained, logical, habitual reasons. You do things because they're comfortable and you can eliminate surprise. The choice of the left path can also symbolize a wish to return to the past or a need to work on things from your past at this time.

If you've chosen the right path, then you're moving into the unknown. You're at a point in your life where you feel adventuresome, ready to try a different way. You're much more interested in tomorrow than you are in yesterday. If you have imagined a fork with three choices (or more!), you could be telling yourself that there are many options out there for you—too many, perhaps, if you found it difficult to make a choice.

Which of your senses predominates? Were all of your senses truly alert or was one sense more dominant? Was the sense of sight most acute? If so, it could indicate that you generally need to be shown things; perhaps you often respond to people with "I see." If sound was the dominant sense, you could be some one who looks consciously for harmony in the world around you; your catch phrase could be, "I hear you." Did anybody in the dream walk want to reach out and touch things, the leaves, the grass, the trees? You could be a person who needs to be in the middle of what's going on, not at all happy to just stand on the sidelines and look and listen. By looking at how your senses functioned in this dream walk, you will become aware of which sense is most effective for you in communicating to your unconscious.

How do you react to the forest? In dreams, a forest is often a symbol for the dreamer's state of confusion. Examine the forest you entered on your walk. Was it dense and thick, growing darker as you moved farther into it? Or was it open and airy, with lots of sunlight filtering down and an easy, open path to follow? Again, your answer can show you how you perceive the world around you at this time.

One dream walker told us that she didn't want to go into the forest at all. She was very anxious about this, and, when she looked down at her feet, she was wearing shoes from her childhood. Our sense was that the forest was bringing a childhood fear back into her mind of being closed in and lost.

What is chasing you? Ah, yes. The creature. What did you see? Was it a person or an animal? Was it a familiar creature or a stranger? Whichever it was, you can proceed as if this were an actual dream, and find two or three attributes you associate with that person or animal. This will give shape to whatever might seem to be "after you" in your real life.

For example, if it was a bear, and you associate unpredictable, uncontrollable anger or bad temper with bears, your unconscious could be telling you that your own temper is a problem. If the animal was a lion or a leopard, you may be approaching problems by stalking them, holding your strength ready to pounce on whatever faces you. Some people see horses—a white stallion has occasionally been encountered on this path. Such an animal shows the importance you place on freedom and your own individuality.

Was the creature a person? If it was a stranger, you may be signaling a general insecurity, self-doubt, a lack of self-esteem. If you could identify the person, what were the attributes you gave for him or her? Just as with the animals discussed above, the prominent characteristic or attribute you give for the person can help you see what is causing anxiety or fear in your life. You may have some real anxieties about your work situation or about authority figures in general which need to be examined. Is your boss chasing you? Is your spouse after you?

Perhaps you didn't see an animal or a person but rather some elusive formless creature made of smoke. You could be signaling that you feel unsure about what is out there; the unknown and all it signifies is on your mind. As you can see, the shape your pursuer takes can provide information about what you unconsciously see as a problem in your life.

Why is it following you? The answer to this question clarifies or reinforces the information you received from the preceding question. If the chaser answers, "Because you are invading my territory," perhaps this means that you are taking on something that you aren't ready for. Or it may show that you have a tendency to control others rather than to gain control of your own life.

Sometimes participants see a very threatening creature, but when this creature answers the question "Why are you chasing me?" the dreamer is often reassured. "Because I can trust you," lets you know that you've begun to be more giving in your relationships; you are learning to trust. "To get to know you better" could show you that you have a need for companionship.

What is your weapon? Now, once you saw the creature, you were asked to use a weapon to vanquish it. Of course, some of you didn't need to actually *use* the weapon, since the creature you saw turned out not to be a threat to you. But what did you brandish? Let's give a few examples of possible weapons and what they might reveal. A stick or tree limb? You could be forcing an issue in your life. A spear or knife? You might use sharp, cutting words as a weapon. A gun? This shows a tendency to use sex as a weapon. A net? Your tactics are to restrain, entrap, surround. Your bare hands? You see yourself as defenseless, unarmed. Did you use reason by saying, for example, "But I love you—don't hurt me"? Your policy is loving confrontation.

What is the gift that is given to you? Did the creature give you a Christmas present, but you didn't open it up? There's something ahead for you—and you appear to be a little hesitant to discover what it is. The buck gave you a piece of its antler? Your gift is a sharing of yourself, so love without fear. Flowers? You are being given a gift of beauty and sensitivity from yourself—stop and smell the roses. Treasure box? A large diamond ring? There are jewels within yourself (with a diamond being the most valuable) that you can fall back on when you need to.

At what point do you feel fear? To what extent are you fearful? These two questions can be discussed together. Were you frightened after the first noise? Are you at a point in your life where you don't feel you have much control over your situation—or some aspect of it—so that most surprises seem to be unpleasant ones? This could be reflected in your reaction to the noise. Do you normally approach things negatively, assuming that each new situation is going to be a fearful or unpleasant one. As we noted earlier, just the fact that you find yourself in a dark thick forest can invoke fear. The forest can represent a dense, impenetrable set of obstacles that you confront in real life. You may not see a way through or around this dense forest.

Others, however, may feel simple curiosity. Based on your particular reaction, you can learn much about your life and perhaps how to take steps to alleviate some fears.

We hope that you have learned something about yourself that you might not have been aware of through this dream walk. But we also hope that you have seen, in a sort of "dream laboratory," how dreams themselves work to give you this same kind of information—as well as the guidance to deal with what is happening in your life.

Lucid Dreaming

Lucid dreaming is just what the term implies: being aware during a dream that it is a dream and using that awareness to shape and direct the dream. This technique can be used to pull yourself out of a nightmarish dream situation or even turn that situation into something positive. You can also use it to help focus on what's important in the dream: an action, a symbol, something you have missed in earlier dreams on the same topic.

Near the end of our writing this book, Pat Shepherd got in her car one evening, fumbled around in the dark a minute or two before she found her keys, and finally got the right one in the ignition. At exactly the moment when she turned the car engine on—and with it, the car radio—she heard the word "…dreamwork" come from the speakers. She was pleased at the synchronicity and serendipity of this moment.

As she continued to listen, she realized she had tuned into the middle of an interview with a musician who was talking about how he works on new compositions in his dreams. The musician said that he will often compose a work in a dream, pause in the middle of the creative session, go and get the electric harp on which he plays his music, and then come back into the dream and play the music. Later, when he wakes up, he can remember what he has created and play it during recording sessions.

We want to stress that, when we say that he "gets the electric harp," "comes back into the dream," and "plays the music," we don't mean that he actually wakes up, gets out of bed, and physically picks up the instrument. Rather, he puts the dream on a sort of "freeze-frame," mentally prepares to play the harp, starts the dream going again, and, in his dream, plays the new music. Thus, when he wakes up, he has had a vivid session with the song, and he is able to retain it in memory to use later.

Lucid dreaming can provide the opportunity for achieving a high state of creativity: what Ann Faraday, in her book *The Dream Game*, calls "a higher state of consciousness reflecting an actual coming together of head and heart...."

Ms. Faraday and most others who work with dreams see lucid dreaming as serving an even more important function: helping us to deal with less pleasant dreams, dreams in which we are chased by some monster or are in a terrifying or dangerous situation. These dreams come to help us deal with the events and happenings of our lives which are causing us anxiety and fear on a daily basis. Lucid dreaming allows us to become aware, when such dreams are happening to us, that we are indeed in a dream. Then we can begin to take control of the situation, direct its outcome in one way or another, and take from the experience emotional comfort as well as knowledge that we can use to handle the situation in our waking life.

Lucid dreaming can occur no matter what type of dream one is having. It often happens spontaneously as the dreamer approaches fear, anxiety, truth, or denial about his or her situation. The dreamer is coming too close to the conscious mind, which rebels by allowing the dreamer to take control of the dream. As with all other dreams, the key is to remember and record these lucid incidents for study. The more understood they are, they more useful this technique can be in dreams, and the more often you will choose it.

Let's look at how this technique can be used. Imagine a dream in which we are walking in a dark alley; as we walk, we become conscious that someone—or something—is following us. We start to run, but so does the pursuer! We soon realize that it is gaining on us, and the alley in front of us is getting longer, and there seems to be no way to avoid being caught, and—well, who knows what awful thing may be about to happen to us.

Normally, such a dream just continues until we wake up, or until we wake ourselves up because all we want is to escape the situation. Our emotions when we awake are very strong ones of fear, anxiety, and confusion.

But with lucid dreaming, we become aware that this is, in fact, "only" a dream. Instead of running away from the person or thing which is chasing us, we suddenly stop, turn around, and confront it. If we are truly lucid, truly aware that this is a dream, we will also know that whatever is happening cannot really hurt us. So we are perfectly safe in letting the monster catch up with us. More importantly, we are then in a position to see what the monster actually is. As most of us know, the unknown can be terribly frightening. As soon as we discover what is lying in wait for us, our hearts start to slow down, we begin to recover our senses, and we can pull together our defenses and actually deal with the problem. Until that time, though, we can only worry—or panic.

Yes, you say, but now that we are facing this—this Thing—what do we do next? Well, we can begin with reason. We can ask why this creature is chasing us. There's a good chance we'll get an answer. For example, "You dropped your glasses. I just want to return them." Here, the monster simply wants to help us see the truth. Or the thing chasing us turns out to be someone from the past who evokes extreme guilt whenever we see or think of this person. "Forgive yourself," says this monster. "Release the old pain and go on."

But what if we don't get an answer to our question? What if the monster continues to come at us? We might decide to arm ourselves. Assuming we are successful in our defense, we would then want to do a bit of a post-mortem on our monster. It wouldn't answer our original question, but we could try to discover what this monster represented and also what the chosen weapon represented. (Look it up in your Living Dictionary.)

However, there is yet another option. If the monster won't answer our questions and continues to come after us, we can simply stand our ground and let it do the worst it can to us. After all, *it is only a dream.* We cannot be hurt, so we can face our worst fears and learn just exactly what will result. If the monster chasing us turns out to be our fear of losing our job, perhaps one of the most valuable experiences we can have is to face this possibility. In a dream, we can let the monster reach us, grab us, chew us up, and spit us out. When it has finished with us, we can take stock. Almost certainly, we will find that we have survived, and we can look around and decide what to do next.

When we wake up from such an experience, instead of the unpleasant feelings of fear and anxiety, we experience much more positive feelings. We have a sense that we can survive the worst. We are able to move beyond the anxiety and perhaps look at some of our options. Maybe at lunch today, we could call Elaine over at the TV network and check out some job possibilities. Or perhaps it's time to look into freelancing in our field. After all these years we've got a lot of knowledge, experience, contacts, and...

We offer one caution here. It is sometimes tempting to take over in a dream and force a happy outcome without stopping to understand the source of the monster—our fear. Simply confronting the monster, blasting it away somehow, and then walking off into the sunset would not teach us much. How we got into the situation in the first place is important. How to handle the situation in our waking life is even more important. In other words, simply walking into the boss's office and blowing up at her—or worse—will not solve anything. Yet, when we use a lucid dreaming experience to *force* a happy ending on our situation, whatever it may be, that is really all we are doing. We have not allowed ourselves the opportunity to recognize more effective measures that may be available to us.

If we allow the ego to take control of our dream, we're watering down or distorting the valid information which our Master Teacher has for us. If, on the other hand, we can stop a cycle of nightmarish dreams without giving control to the ego, then lucid dreaming can be helpful.

Past-Life Dreams

Once in a great while, there are dreams which defy understanding. No matter how carefully we work with the symbols and situations in the dream, we just don't get that "Aha!" sense. Sometimes, as we've said, the dream can be one that was given to us for someone else who wasn't ready to receive it. But what about dreams that are about us, not about someone else, but which we still can't figure out? One possible answer is that such a dream could be about us in a past life! This is especially true if the dream truly seems to represent a particular historical era, filled with period costumes and surroundings. Another clue is that we don't recognize a person's face but we *know* that the person is Aunt Sue, with whom we are now having a relationship problem.

As we've said, the unconscious has a huge warehouse of material from which it can construct the dreams it presents each night; included in that warehouse is material from our past, including other lives we may have lived.

We worked many years ago with a newly married couple. They both came from previous marriages and had a number of children from those relationships. The wife was anxious to adopt yet another child; the husband was not. In addition, they were contemplating buying land in the Rockies. These are the things we knew they were working on at the time the wife brought us the following dream:

> *I dreamed I was an American Indian woman, pregnant, dressed in rough leather clothes and moccasins. I vividly remember that my outer cover or blanket was made of some kind of animal skin; I remember its touch and especially its smell. I was with my husband who was a mountain man, roughly dressed and carrying a large, old rifle. We were traveling through rugged beautiful mountain country, and I strongly sensed that we were running from something. I soon discovered what it was: a band of mountain men on horseback, who caught up to us and attacked us. There was no way we could defend ourselves; I remember that I was run through with a lance-type of object, and my husband was shot and killed.*

As we said, we worked with this dream at some length, but we could not find its message. There just didn't seem to be any way that the dream was guiding this woman in dealing with her problems. Jim was the one who finally asked if perhaps, because there was so much attention to detail, so much authenticity in the detail, and so much sensory information, the dream was a replay of an actual experience from a past life. Because none of us wanted to give up on the dream, we decided to give this theory a try.

We continued to stick with the idea that all dreams are guidance dreams. How, we asked, could a dream from a past life provide this woman with guidance? First of all, if we assumed that the dream was a past-life experience, it would help to explain her obsession with wanting to adopt a baby. As a matter of fact, once we had decided to take this tack with the dream, the wife told us that she had always wanted to adopt an American Indian baby. We could see why, since the pregnancy was not completed in the dream. Another point the dream helped to clarify was the couple's strong desire to buy land in the Rockies. The dream made their love for the area obvious, even though they had had such a bad experience at the end of their lives there.

Finally, we saw that their relationship in that wild earlier time had been cut short, before they had had time to start a family or work through the things that most couples have to deal with in a marriage. We all saw that it was quite possible that these two had come together again in this life in order to continue and develop the relationship as they had not been able to before. When we brought out this point, we got a great "Aha!" from both the dreamer and her husband—this was a most enlightening piece of information for them, as it explained shared fears and desires.

Though such dreams are extremely rare, we have found that they do occur. As we have stressed, we first work very hard to be absolutely sure that we cannot explain the dream by the usual methods. However, on the rare occasions when this is not fruitful and the dream appears to be presenting an experience from an earlier age, we have found that we can derive invaluable information from considering the dream in this new light. We need to ask such questions as: "Why did I receive this information now? How does it tie into a present growth pattern?"

Dreaming for Others

You may remember the "Sonja Henie" dream from Chapter 4, in which Pat received a dream for her friend Dottie. There are times when other people, usually close friends or relatives, may come to us for a special kind of help. They are working on a serious problem, involving career, relationship, health, or whatever.

They know they are receiving guidance, but they have not been able to remember their dreams—they're blocking the messages, out of fear or denial. In such cases, people have come to Pat and asked her to have a dream for them.

Now, this may sound like a strange request, but many dream workers have had successful experiences dreaming for others. Three very important require-ments must be met for the process to be effective. First, you must have been asked by the other person to receive the dream. It is not up to you to judge someone else's situation, decide that he or she needs your help, and then request a dream for the other person. No matter how loving your motives may be, such an action is *always* interference unless you have been asked to help in this way. However, if a friend or family member feels that dream guidance is being blocked for one reason or another, that person may wish to come to you for help. *Only under this condition* should you ask to have a dream for another person.

The second requirement is that you yourself must be able to put aside whatever you are working on. If this sounds like you need to ask permission of your unconscious, that's exactly right. We'll illustrate this step shortly.

The third requirement is that you must request dream guidance that is in the person's highest good. You do not necessarily know what that highest good may be, so this step, like the first one, ensures that you and your perceptions stay out of the way of the message. You must not in any way interfere the guidance that comes through.

Pat has developed a procedure she uses whenever she is asked to receive or remember a dream for someone else.

꒰   ꒱

After I finish my nightly routine, I first ask my unconscious if I might take a break from working on my own problems tonight. If I feel reassured that I can catch up on my own work later, I take this as an affirmative answer from my unconscious. Then I call the name of the person who has asked for help. I call that name two or three times, asking that the lines of communication be open between us, and that I may be allowed to receive information that is in that person's best interest or highest good in this situation. Finally, I conclude by saying, "Thank you, Father!"

&

We should note that sometimes the request from the other person is made at an unconscious level. A good example of that is the Sonja Henie dream. In this case, as you remember, Pat's friend Dottie was blocking guidance from her own unconscious that she needed medical attention. But her higher self was on the job and brought the dream to Pat, who was very close to Dottie and would have been very concerned. On an unconscious level, Pat evidently agreed that this was the most important message which she, Pat, could have received that night, and the dream was allowed to come through to her.

And Finally...

We hope we have shown you the invaluable capacity for dreams to aid us in our lives. Whether we seek guidance for ourselves or for our loved ones, dreams provide a constant wealth of enlightening information . . . if we are willing to pay attention. When interpreted correctly, these gems of the unconscious yield solutions to physical, emotional, mental, and spiritual conditions. Truths are revealed, warnings are conveyed, and help is provided, whether involving finances, relationships, or our moral and spiritual natures.

The primary purpose of this book has been to convince you of the need to open that special delivery letter from your unconscious or higher self, read it, and interpret its meaning. The guidance each of us receives from these messages will make the journey along our life path so much easier, so much clearer—the guidance is ours for the taking.

The real beauty of personal dream interpretaion is that you become your own guide. You are a self-contained resource, both for information about yourself *and* counsel for your life decisions. Indeed, if more people truly listened to their dream messages, many therapists would need to consider new professions!

We are grateful for the opportunity you have given us to provide assistance on your new journey. For in assisting you, we are in turn assisting ourselves. As we read in *The Aquarian Gospel of Jesus the Christ*:

> *There is no lonely Pilgrim on the Way to Light.*
> *[We] only gain the heights by helping*
> *others gain the heights.*

7 | REFERENCES: SOME GOOD BOOKS...

All three of us have been interested in and involved with dreams and dream interpretation for many years, and we have searched out and read much of the material on the subject. Readers are encouraged to do the same, since our book has its own focus and cannot deal comprehensively with all aspects of dream interpretation.

To help in that task, we have prepared a bibliography of some of the works we have found most helpful, along with some notes explaining their particular value. The list is not intended to be comprehensive, but it's a start....

Auras by Edgar Cayce, Virginia Beach, Virginia: A.R.E. Press, 1945.

Though not about dreams, this book gives great insight into the meanings of colors as they may be used in dreams.

Breakthrough Dreaming: How to Tap the Power of Your 24-Hour Mind, by Gayle Delaney, Ph. D., New York: Bantam Books, 1991.

Filled with fascinating dreams and their interpretation using a helpful interview technique.

Creative Dreaming by Patricia Garfield, Ph.D., New York: Ballantine Books, 1974.

This book gives a good multi-cultural look at dreams and shows how to use them in unique ways.

A Dictionary of Symbols by J.E. Cirlot (translated from the Spanish by Jack Sage), Routledge & Kegan Paul Ltd., New York: Philosophical Library, Inc., 1962.

Presents ancient art symbols of the Orient and medieval traditions in the West; includes clarifying studies on universal symbols.

The Dream Game by Dr. Ann Faraday, New York: Perennial Library, Harper & Row, 1974.

One of the first of the modern books on interpreting dreams, including the use of a dream diary—she emphasizes the humor and lightheartedness often found in dreams.

Dream Power by Dr. Ann Faraday, New York: Berkley Books, 1972.

An excellent eclectic and practical guide to dreams by this very insightful British author.

Dream Symbolism by Manly P. Hall, Los Angeles: The Philosophical Research Society, Inc., 1965.

A handbook on sleep phenomena; includes indicators of personality problems, use of dreams in psychotherapy, and emphasis on the wisdom of the subconscious.

Dreams and Healing: A Succinct and Lively Interpretation of Dreams by John A. Sanford, New York: John A. Paulist Press, 1978.

Some very good information on the history and application of dreams, as well as two longitudinal studies of the dreams of two individuals.

Dreams: The Language of the Unconscious (revised edition) by Edgar Cayce, Hugh Linn, Tom C. Clark, Shane Miller, and W. N. Petersen, Virginia Beach, Virginia: A.R.E. Press, 1971.

An excellent introduction to dream symbology and the importance of seeking spiritual guidance in interpreting dreams.

Dreams: Your Magic Mirror by Elsie Sechrist, with interpretations of Edgar Cayce, New York: Warner Books, 1968. [Out of print.]

An excellent book on dreams which gives some helpful hints on interpreting dreams technically as well as symbolically. The material is largely from Edgar Cayce.

Edgar Cayce on Dreams by Harmon H. Bro, Ph.D., New York: Warner Books, 1968. Edited by Hugh Lynn Cayce.

A book filled with good information on dreams, but especially fascinating are the interpretations by Edgar Cayce.

How to Interpret Your Dreams: Practical Techniques Based on the Edgar Cayce Readings by Mark A.Thurston, Ph. D., Virginia Beach, Virginia: A.R.E. Press, 1978.

An overall treatment of dreams and dreaming from the Edgar Cayce material.

The Jungian-Senoi Dreamwork Manual: A Step-by-Step Introduction to Working with Dreams by Strephon Kaplan-Williams, Novato, California: Journey Press, 1988.

Uses Jungian principles as well as dream techniques developed by the Senoi people of Malaysia—the so-called "dream" people—to present thirty-five methods for interpreting dreams.

Lacandon Dream Symbolism (Volume I: Dream Symbolism and Interpretation; Volume II: Dictionary, Index and Classification of Dream Symbols) by Robert D. Bruce, Perugino, Mexico: Ediciones EuroAmericanas, Klaus Thiele, 1979.

This hard-to-find book presents a fascinating look at the Lacandon Mayan Indians of Chiapas, Mexico, for whom dreaming is a central act of daily life; discusses clairvoyance, telepathy, and the tribe's unique use of Ancient Mayan dream symbols.

A Little Course in Dreams by Robert Bosnak, Boston: Shambhala Publications, Inc, 1988.

A small book showing by example how to use Jungian principles, individually or in groups, for dream interpretation.

Living Your Dreams by Gayle Delaney, Ph.D., San Francisco: Harper & Row, 1988.

A very practical guide to using your dreams to solve everyday problems. Well-researched and written.

Lucid Dreaming: Dawning of the Clear Light by Gregory Scott Sparrow, Virginia Beach, Virginia: A.R.E. Press, 1976.

Based on the Edgar Cayce Readings. Explains the technique of lucid dreaming and how to use it effectively in one's dream life.

The Meaning in Dreams and Dreaming by Maria F. Mahoney, Secaucus, New Jersey: The Citadel Press, 1966.

Explains the techniques of Carl Jung in everyday language to help others understand the meanings of their dreams.

Meditation—Gateway to Light by Elsie Sechrist, Virginia Beach, Virginia: A.R.E. Press, 1972.

Based on the Edgar Cayce Readings, this is an outstanding guide to meditation as a way to establish communication with the unconscious mind.

A Return to Love: Reflections on the Principles of "A Course in Miracles" by Marianne Williamson, New York: Harper Collins, 1992.

A gifted interpreter of the material in A Course in Miracles. She is able to state its principles with clarity and simplicity, providing us spiritual food for our spiritual search.

Symbols and the Self (revised edition) by Violet Shelley, Virginia Beach, Virginia: A.R.E. Press, 1976.

Excellent material on the symbolic meaning of numbers and planets in dreams.

Waking Dreams by Mary M. Watkins, New York: Harper Colophon Books, Harper & Row, 1976.

Provides a good historical background on the use of fantasy. Shows how daydreams may be interpreted using the techniques for regular dreams.

You Can Heal Your Life by Louise L. Hay, Santa Monica: Hay House, 1984.

Includes some very interesting material on the use of dreams in dealing with physical and health problems.

DREAM JOURNAL

DATE: _____

GUIDANCE QUESTION: _____

WAKING EMOTIONS: _____

_____

DREAM TITLE: _____

DREAM: _____

_____

_____

_____

_____

_____

_____

_____

_____

_____

_____

RECENT CONCERNS: _____

_____

_____

SETTING:

UNUSUAL DETAILS:

STATEMENTS/QUESTIONS/ANSWERS:

SYMBOLS AT WORK:

DREAM MESSAGE:

DATE: _____

GUIDANCE QUESTION: _____

WAKING EMOTIONS: _____

_____

DREAM TITLE: _____

DREAM: _____

_____

_____

_____

_____

_____

_____

_____

_____

_____

_____

_____

RECENT CONCERNS: _____

_____

_____

SETTING:

UNUSUAL DETAILS:

_____

_____

_____

STATEMENTS/QUESTIONS/ANSWERS:

_____

_____

SYMBOLS AT WORK:

_____

_____

_____

_____

_____

DREAM MESSAGE:

_____

_____

_____

_____

_____

DATE:

GUIDANCE QUESTION:

WAKING EMOTIONS:

DREAM TITLE:

DREAM:

RECENT CONCERNS:

SETTING: _____

UNUSUAL DETAILS: _____

_____

_____

_____

STATEMENTS/QUESTIONS/ANSWERS: _____

_____

_____

SYMBOLS AT WORK: _____

_____

_____

_____

_____

_____

DREAM MESSAGE: _____

_____

_____

_____

_____

_____

DATE: _____

GUIDANCE QUESTION: _____

WAKING EMOTIONS: _____

_____

DREAM TITLE: _____

DREAM: _____

_____

_____

_____

_____

_____

_____

_____

_____

_____

_____

_____

RECENT CONCERNS: _____

_____

_____

SETTING:

UNUSUAL DETAILS:

STATEMENTS/QUESTIONS/ANSWERS:

SYMBOLS AT WORK:

DREAM MESSAGE:

DATE:

GUIDANCE QUESTION:

WAKING EMOTIONS:

DREAM TITLE:

DREAM:

RECENT CONCERNS:

SETTING:
_____

UNUSUAL DETAILS:
_____
_____
_____
_____

STATEMENTS/QUESTIONS/ANSWERS:
_____
_____
_____

SYMBOLS AT WORK:
_____
_____
_____
_____
_____
_____
_____

DREAM MESSAGE:
_____
_____
_____
_____
_____

Date:

Guidance question:

Waking emotions:

Dream title:

Dream:

Recent concerns:

SETTING:

UNUSUAL DETAILS:

STATEMENTS/QUESTIONS/ANSWERS:

SYMBOLS AT WORK:

DREAM MESSAGE:

DATE:

GUIDANCE QUESTION:

WAKING EMOTIONS:

DREAM TITLE:

DREAM:

RECENT CONCERNS:

SETTING: _____

UNUSUAL DETAILS: _____

_____

_____

_____

STATEMENTS/QUESTIONS/ANSWERS: _____

_____

_____

SYMBOLS AT WORK: _____

_____

_____

_____

_____

_____

DREAM MESSAGE: _____

_____

_____

_____

_____

_____

DATE:

GUIDANCE QUESTION:

WAKING EMOTIONS:

DREAM TITLE:

DREAM:

RECENT CONCERNS:

SETTING: _____

UNUSUAL DETAILS: _____

_____

_____

_____

STATEMENTS/QUESTIONS/ANSWERS: _____

_____

_____

SYMBOLS AT WORK: _____

_____

_____

_____

_____

_____

DREAM MESSAGE: _____

_____

_____

_____

_____

_____

DATE:

GUIDANCE QUESTION:

WAKING EMOTIONS:

DREAM TITLE:

DREAM:

RECENT CONCERNS:

SETTING:

UNUSUAL DETAILS:

STATEMENTS/QUESTIONS/ANSWERS:

SYMBOLS AT WORK:

DREAM MESSAGE:

PHOTO BY TOM KARONIKA

About the Authors

Pat and Jim Fregia have studied dreams and worked with dream interpretation for more than 20 years. Better known as the *Dream Team* in the southwest Texas area they call home, the two have presented numerous dream seminars and workshops. Since 1986, they have appeared regularly on Houston radio and TV. They have also published several articles in *Venture Inward*, the journal of the Association for Research & Enlightenment (A.R.E.). The Fregias can be contatcted for assistance in dream interpretation at Box 52, Tagosa Springs, CO 81147, or by phone at (303) 731-2797.